VOL. 2 — INTERMEDIATE TECHNIQUES OF JUJITSU — THE GENTLE ART

by
George Kirby

Editor: Mike Lee
Graphic Design: Karen Massad

Art Production:
Junko Sadjadpour
Amy Goldman Koss

Photography: Mario Prado

Eighteenth printing 2005

WARNING

This book is presented only as a means of preserving a unique aspect of the heritage of the martial arts. Neither Ohara Publications nor the author makes any representation, warranty or guarantee that the techniques described or illustrated in this book will be safe or effective in any self-defense situation or otherwise. You may be injured if you apply or train in the techniques of self-defense illustrated in this book, and neither Ohara Publications nor the author is responsible for any such injury that may result. It is essential that you consult a physician regarding whether or not to attempt any technique described in this book. Specific self-defense responses illustrated in this book may not be justified in any particular situation in view of all of the circumstances or under the applicable federal, state or local law. Neither Ohara Publications nor the author makes any representation or warranty regarding the legality or appropriateness of any technique mentioned in this book.

BLACK BELT BOOKS
A Division of **OHARA ⦿ PUBLICATIONS, INC.**
World Leader in Martial Arts Publications

ACKNOWLEDGEMENTS

A technical manual of this sort can never be considered the sole creation of one person. There were many people who assisted and supported me in this endeavor in one way or another. I would like to take this opportunity to mention their names and thank them for their assistance:

Yudansha Kevin Harte and Mudansha Randall Thomas for their assistance in demonstrating the techniques in this book;

Professor Sanzo Jack Seki, my original instructor for many years, who asked supportingly if I was going to come out with a second book;

Professor Harold Brosious and other top yudansha across the United States who enjoyed my first book and thus encouraged me to go on;

Adel, my wife, who understood the importance to me of writing these books to spread the art, and has thus been very supportive;

The purchasers across the country who gave me their opinions of my first book and suggestions for a second book; and finally

The staff at Ohara Publications for having the faith in me to publish my first book and for going ahead with the second to further enhance the mudansha's skill and growth in the art.

Thanks to all. I couldn't have done this without any of them.

—*George Kirby*

ABOUT THE AUTHOR

George Kirby has been a serious student, teacher and proponent of jujitsu since his introduction to the art in the early 1960s. Kirby was awarded a shodan in 1968 from Sanzo Seki. In 1969, he and his associate, Bill Fromm, formed the American Ju-Jitsu Association. Kirby currently serves as the AJA's president and chairman of its board of directors.

A native of Los Angeles, Kirby earned his bachelor of arts and master of arts degrees in Social Science at California State University, Los Angeles, in 1969. He also secured his state teaching credentials during that time and is now a high school instructor with the Los Angeles City Schools.

Kirby has actively taught jujitsu and basic self-defense from 1968-75 at the Burbank YMCA and since 1974 for the Burbank Parks and Recreation Department. He has taught self-defense courses for teachers in the Los Angeles City Schools as well as designed and conducted a very successful jujitsu/self-defense program for students from 1974 through 1983. He was awarded the 1981 AAU Jujitsu National Sports Award, a certificate of honor from the Federation of Practicing Ju-Jutsuans, and was voted Outstanding Instructor in both 1971 and 1974 by the California Branch Ju-jitsu Federation. He was promoted to rokudan in 1985. He is also the United States' representative for the European Ju-Jitsu Union and International Jujitsu/Tai-Federation.

Kirby has written numerous articles for BLACK BELT magazine, and has authored three editions of *Budoshin Ju-Jitsu*, a comprehensive compilation of jujitsu techniques used as a workbook in many jujitsu classes. He is also the author of *Jujitsu: Basic Techniques of the Gentle Art,* published by Ohara Publications in 1983. In addition to his normal instructional responsibilities, Kirby also conducts numerous martial arts clinics, offers instruction in the use of the hanbo, yawarra stick (*koshi no bo*), and jutte. He is also an active organizer and judge at tournament competitions.

When not spending time on jujitsu or his teaching profession, Kirby enjoys gardening, photography, traveling, and spending time with his wife, Adel.

PREFACE

Two Inseparable Friends

Control is the key.
Patience is the key.
The key is not trying at all.
Self-control is the key.
Ki is the key to success.

Control is the ki.
Patience is the ki.
The ki is not trying at all.
Self-control is the ki.
Ki is the ki to success.

In writing *Jujitsu: Basic Techniques of the Gentle Art,* I had the opportunity to present some of the basic history, theory, and philosophy of jujitsu. Some time was spent on what *ki* was and how it was used. The circle theory was explained; that all actions have a logical consequence and that the use of ki was an essential element of the theory. The basic mechanics of the art were also explained; how techniques should be practiced and executed, what attitude should be maintained, and how theory should be applied to the learning of techniques.

I also had the opportunity to present the history and philosophy of the art. Through research it was established that jujitsu was in existence over 2,500 years ago, making it one of the oldest martial arts. The historical growth of jujitsu was established as were the various routes it took to the Western world. Philosophically, I tried to present the philosophy of the art as taught by my two instructors as well as using additional study done on my own. I presented my thoughts as clearly as possible; that knowledge meant responsibility, confidence could be equated with humility, and that any sort of violence goes against the basic precepts of the art.

The preceding poem is very simple to understand on the surface and the comments appear to be self-evident. However, there is much more below the surface, especially when both sides are compared line for line and in their totality. What appears to be simple on the surface becomes more and more complex as one probes deeper. It's not confusing though—only more complex.

The same is true with jujitsu. As one's knowledge of the art increases, a serious student will find that there is more to the art than what initially meets the eye. As knowledge is mastered, new questions and possibilities come into being. *Jujitsu: Intermediate Techniques of the Gentle Art* will attempt to broaden the knowledge of the intermediate student who has progressed through the first book. I hope this book will help the student acquire more knowledge and a greater understanding of the art while opening more doors of inquiry at the same time.   —G.K.

INTRODUCTION

Jujitsu is an ancient martial art that encompasses three of today's more popular *do* (ways): *judo, aikido,* and *karatedo.* While *Jujitsu: Basic Techniques of the Gentle Art* provided basic information in the areas of history, theory, philosophy, and mechanics of the art, *Jujitsu: Intermediate Techniques of the Gentle Art* will provide additional theoretical background as well as numerous additional techniques. These are designed to serve as a foundation for bringing the serious student to the level of *shodan* (first degree black belt).

This book provides advanced theoretical concepts dealing with multiple attackers, maneuvering strategies, developing variations, and combinations of basic moves and techniques, and the application of standing techniques to ground situations. The philosophical testing concepts for the higher ranks of brown belt through shodan are discussed. In contrast to the first book, Japanese terminology is used in this text. Thus, a brief discussion of its use is presented as well as a basic Japanese/English glossary and index of techniques. Time is devoted to a further clarification and explanation of a *complete* jujitsu technique. Brown and black belt requirements as established by the American Ju-Jitsu Association are shown. And in addition to this material, a cross-reference chart indexing various attacks to the techniques is offered in this book.

This book will help you grow beyond my first book by allowing you to become more knowledgeable in the art. Not only does this book have different techniques and variations, but the student is encouraged to combine basic techniques, as in the first book, so as to create entirely different combinations or variations of techniques. In this way you will truly grow as a student of the art.

I'd like to remind the reader to use extreme caution when practicing the techniques shown in this book. Refer to the safety rules in the first book and be considerate of your *uke* (partner). Be aware that jujjitsu techniques are designed to cause pain, discomfort, and possibly severe injury. Carelessness is no excuse when working with another human being. You must be considerate of your partner or an injury will be the inevitable result.

Practicing any martial art also requires that your body be loosened up. This is particularly true of jujitsu. You should engage in stretching exercises to loosen and warm up your body. Exercises need not be done for the purpose of developing muscles and strength. Neither of these are essential in jujitsu; but a loose, relaxed body *is*. Particular attention should be given to loosening and stretching the joints of your body, particularly your neck, wrist, and ankles.

You should also be aware that this book has certain limitations. It can provide the technical basics as well as the theoretical, historical, and philosophical knowledge that goes with the art. Even though *Jujitsu: Intermediate Techniques of the Gentle Art* can provide a lot of material, there are some things that it simply cannot do. It can't show all of the possible variations of techniques. It cannot develop a self-defense system designed just for you. It cannot recreate a dojo situation with the all-important student/instructor relationship. It can't develop your attitude or measure all of the areas in which you should be evaluated. Most critical: it cannot test you for shodan.

There are some things you can do that will help compensate for some of the limitations mentioned. You can work on developing a positive attitude in as many areas mentioned in the text as possible. You are encouraged to experiment with techniques to discover additional combinations and variations using the five-step process also mentioned in the text. You must train with a positive mind, seeking to gain knowledge, rather than just working for a specific belt rank.

Continue down the road of learning. This book should help you broaden your knowledge of the art of jujitsu. Once the techniques in this book and my first one are mastered, you will find that your knowledge can grow geometrically. You will, as explained later on, realize why jujitsu is an endless learning experience. Keep an open and positive mind. Grow with the art. You'll discover that you'll also grow as a person. After all, that's what the art is supposed to do. —*G.K.*

CONTENTS

CHAPTER 1

Use of Japanese Terminology

The world would be a simple place to live in if we all spoke the same language. Unfortunately we don't. Our world is a Tower of Babel. A country may have one language or many, one dialect or several, and idiosyncracies or local slangs that can create confusion among the unaware.

The same problem occurs with Japanese-English terminology in the martial arts. It's amazing how many ways the same thing can be said in English—and Japanese. There are also a variety of ways in which the terms used in the martial arts come into being. Some arts use terms that deal directly with the physical motion of the *tori* (defender) or *uke* attacker). Others use more artistic names for techniques that may sound totally unrelated to those unschooled in that art. Some systems in the U.S. use only Japanese terminology and some use only English. When the two meet it can be very confusing.

I'll be the first to admit that my exposure to the Japanese language has been very limited. This is simply a statement of fact. When I first studied under Professor Sanzo Seki all of the terminology was in Japanese. Seki Sensei would give an English translation if an upper rank asked for such. During the years I studied under him, he was under increased pressure to use English and, as he instructed at the facility of a community service agency, he had to comply to some extent. Nevertheless, higher ranking students grew to prefer the Japanese over English. Perhaps part of this was due to our desire to know more about the art. I'm also inclined to believe that as we understood more of the Japanese terminology, it seemed to make more sense and was easier to follow than the English.

Professor Seki tended to use what I and others call *generic* terminology. These are general terms that refer to specific types of techniques, often including all the variations of the basic techniques. There were also times when specific techniques had specific names—but they still made more sense in Japanese. The generic terminology was broken down into two general areas. It either referred to actions in reference to movement by the tori or the uki. How the Japanese terms were put together usually gave us an idea of what the technique's name was in reference to.

After studying with Professor Seki for a number of years I then had the opportunity to study Ketsugo jujitsu under Professor Harold Brosious. The Ketsugo system used only English. The use of English only is no reflection on the effectiveness of the techniques in the system. I mention it only to illustrate that some systems use Japanese and some don't. This did create problems for me in teaching my students, as I incorporated portions of Ketsugo into the original jujitsu I studied under Professor Seki. I felt these additions would enhance the system. It was difficult for me to tell my students that there wasn't a Japanese term for the technique. I could've composed a term, based upon my studies with Professor Seki. I chose not to do so because I realized that my limited knowledge of Japanese might result in incorrect terms. The results might be an insult to the Japanese language, the art, and my instructors, none of which I wished to show any disrespect to.

The English/Japanese problem is not unique to me or the styles of jujitsu I studied. The problem is rampant throughout the martial arts. The same techniques have different names in Japanese *and* English, probably dependent upon the sensei who first put the techniques down in writing, (whether or not he was writing in Japanese or English).

Writing Japanese phonetically for English consumption also added confusion. The following chart is merely the tip of the iceberg in jujitsu:

System:	Japanese (phonetic)	English translation
Budoshin:	*Ippon seol nage*	one-arm hip throw
Danzan-ryu:	*Seoi nage*	flying mare (back carry throw)
Juko-ryu:	*Ippon seoinage*	shoulder throw
Kawaishi:	*Seoie nage*	one arm shoulder throw
Samuari:	*Ippon seoinage*	single arm shoulder throw
Budoshin:	*Tomoe nage*	stomach throw
Danzan-ryu	*Tomoe nage*	high circle throw
Kazwaishi:	*Tomoe nage*	stomach throw (circle throw)
Budoshin:	*Harai goshi*	outer sweeping hip throw
Miyama-ryu:	*Harai goshi*	sweeping loin
Danzan-ryu	*Harai goshi*	loin and ankle sweep
Kawaishi:	*Harai goshi*	sweeping loin (hip) throw

Each grouping indicates the same techniques with different names, variations in spelling or phrasing, all of which can lead to a lot of confusion. Who is to say which one is proper? Probably all are correct.

In this book, the Japanese terminology taught by Professor Seki will be used whenever it's applicable. The appendix glossary has a complete listing of techniques. You should keep in mind that Professor Seki used simple terminology whenever possible. There are also many very similar techniques that may have the same name. There might be several types of *te nage* (hand throw). The subtle differences would usually be in the execution of the technique. Another example of similarities would be in some of the variations of *tomoe nage* (stomach throw). Just a few are:

Sode tomoe nage = sleeve stomach throw

Kubi tomoe nage = neck stomach throw

Kubi shimi tomoe nage = neck-choke stomach throw

Styles in Jujitsu

You might have noticed there were five styles (*ryu*) of jujitsu mentioned previously: Budoshin, Danzan-ryu, Juko-ryu, Kawaishi, and Samurai (to name but a few). Not all of these are necessarily major ryu. Several more could be listed and the list would remain incomplete. Professor Seki felt that there weren't any styles of jujitsu. He maintained that there was only the *art*. He is basically correct. All the styles generally seem to cover the same technical and theoretical material. All the styles have areas of emphasis or specialization. Most of the styles get the mudansha to about the same point by the time he's ready to test for shodan.

One of the problems, perhaps unique to the U.S., is our desire to categorize things and try to point out subtle differences. Perhaps this is one reason why there are so many ryu of the art in the U.S. The problem even surfaced in inquiries about my first book. Readers wanted to know what style of the art was being taught.

I have tried to stress the same philosophy to my students that Seki Sensei did to his—that there are no styles in jujitsu—only the art. For those who insist on a style or ryu, the ryu being presented in this book can be called Budoshin jujitsu.

However, the term *budoshin* really has very little to do with the mechanics of jujitsu. Rather, it expresses an attitude or outlook toward life. It means to live in a respectful and honorable manner. It means to be chivalrous and knightly in one's behavior. As I instruct my students, it is the attitude and philosophy that goes along with the mechanics of the art. It is not an indication of any specific emphasis in technique or form.

As far as the mechanics of Budoshin jujitsu are concerned, the student is presented with complete jujitsu techniques from the outset, as in most styles of the art. Initial techniques may be simple and basic. However, they will enable the student to progress to more complex situations where either more complex techniques or variations are required. There is no particular emphasis in any one of the three *do* (judo, karatedo, and aikido), that are the basis, or more correctly modified *ways* of the art. A student is taught the art as a whole, for that is the way jujitsu should be taught.

BASIC VOCABULARY

Numbers

Ichi	1	Ju-roku	16
Ni	2	Ju-shichi	17
San	3	Ju-hachi	18
Shi, yo, yon	4	Ju-ku	19
Go	5	Ni-ju	20
Roku	6		
Shichi, nanae	7	**Parts of Body**	
Hachi	8	Atama	head
Ku	9	Kao	face
Ju	10	Ago	chin
Ju-ichi	11	Kubi	neck
Ju-ni	12	Ude	arm
Ju-san	13	Hiji or heji	elbow
Ju-shi	14	Te	hand
Ju-go	15	Yubi	fingers

Koshi	hip	Obi	belt
Hiza	knee	Dojo	school
Ashi	foot or leg	Arrigato	thank you
Nodo	throat	Hito	person
Ube	thumb	Sensei	teacher
Karada	body	Undo	workout
Saiki tanden	lower stomach	Jujitsu	power of mind
Mimi	ear	Hiki	pulling
Me	eye	Tsuri	lift or pull up
Tai	body	Sode	sleeve
Mata	thigh	Uke	person receiving technique
Senaka	shoulder	Randori	free exercise
Tekubi	wrist	Harai	outside sweep
		Hane	inside sweep, spring or jump

General Terms

Nage	throw	Kotukai	attention
Kata	form	Rei	bow
Waza	technique	Take	block
Mae	forward	Kobushi	fist
Yoko	sideways	Tsuki	attack
Ushiro	backwards	Kuko	speed
Ukemi	fall	Gyaku	reverse
Nawa	rope	Migi	to the right
Ippon	one point	Hidari	to the left
Ki	wood	Eri	collar
Ki	inner spirit		
Katana	sword		
Onna	woman		
Juji	cross		

AJA Belt Ranks

Kiai	shout	**Dan Grades:**	
Osoto	outer	Shodan	1st Black belt
Otori	throw	Nidan*	2nd
Shiai	contest	Sandan	3rd
Hasami	scissors	Yodan	4th
Shioku	nerves	Godan	5th
Katame	grappling	Rokudan	6th
Shimi	pain, strangling	Shichidan	7th
Tori	person doing technique	Hachidan	8th
Maitta	give up, stop or wait	Kudan	9th
Hai	yes	Judan	10th
Kuruma	wheel		

* *Teaching Certificate required before promotion to Nidan.*

Sara	cupped hand	**Mudansha Grades:**	
Uki	pull, go, float	Rokkyu	6th Green
Otoshi	drop	Gokyu	5th Green/Yellow
Maki	to round	Shikyu	4th Purple
Naka	inner	Sankyu	3rd Brown
Morote	both hands	Nikyu	2nd Brown
Ura	rear	Ikkyu	1st Brown

CHAPTER 2

Advanced Theory

The theories presented in this chapter are designed to enhance and expand upon the the knowledge presented in my first book. With the theoretical knowledge presented here you should be able to develop most of the technical skills required of an intermediate student in the martial art of jujitsu.

Dealing with multiple attackers is a concept that brown belt students should work with and develop through practice. Maneuvering strategies are essential to the advanced student. Understanding and applying them can make your responses totally unpredictable. Developing variations of basic techniques is a third skill essential for a student advancing in the art. Defending yourself on the ground is another area in which an advanced student should develop proficiency. This section will deal with the necessity of *knowing* the art of jujitsu.

Theories don't give you pat answers to problems. Theories can give you only possible solutions, or routes to take to find the solutions. Theories are only relatively valid. If they were absolute, they'd be called laws. Theories work most of the time, but are subject to variations beyond their control. They are not 100 percent true because no one had been able to prove them as such.

The theoretical information presented here is designed to increase your knowledge of the art, and give you the flexibility to develop your skills. It cannot improve your ability a specified amount as its value is determined by your dedication in studying the art.

Maneuvering Strategies

Being able to maneuver in a self-defense situation is one of the most valuable assets in any martial art. It is a skill that requires a thorough understanding of the capabilities of your martial art as well as the potential of your attacker. It requires that you have an understanding of how to avoid being a target as well as the wide variety of targets your attacker may present you with. It also requires that you be able to blend your technical skills with the attack, direction, and momentum of your attacker.

In discussing maneuvering strategies there are three areas that need to be considered: targeting by the attacker, avoidance by the defender, and targeting by the defender. However, before these areas can be discussed they need to be defined.

Targeting *by the attacker* refers to that part of the body the attacker is attempting to attack. Regardless of the attack or weapon an attacker usually goes after one target at a time. If it's a one-two punch to the stomach and face the first target is the stomach and the second is the face. If it's a knife swipe, the target is whatever area the knife may cut along its path. The attacker usually has some idea of what he's doing and what target he's aiming for.

Avoidance by the defender is a fairly obvious response. Basically it means removing yourself or that part of your body as the target. It means doing what you can to get out of the way so that the attack doesn't reach its target.

Targeting *by the defender* is a method by which you respond to the attacker by targeting him. You may execute techniques on him based upon your knowledge, his attack, and the immediate environment. You will usually have a number of targets open to you. You may choose one or more depending upon what you know and what the situation permits.

Once these terms are understood it is easier to discuss maneuvering strategies. We are not going to talk about what techniques can or should be used once maneuvering strategies are executed. We will be talking about how to remove yourself as a target and the varied ways to get close enough to your attacker to do what you want to do.

In a street confrontation you will be targeted by an attacker. He will seek to put you in a position in which his attacks will be most effective. In most situations an attacker's area of maximum effectiveness is relatively narrow. It is usually that area directly in front of him, usually extending a distance of 18-48 inches, the range of effective hits and kicks. *(See Figure 1.)* If he is attacking from behind his range is body contact (as in a bearhug) to 48 inches (as in an extended kick to your back). It might be well to note that if you don't sense an attack coming from behind (except for a grab of any sort), you're not going to be able to do much about it regardless of what you know.

If attacked from the front, the area of maximum danger is about 18-48 inches from the attacker, as previously mentioned. This range, 18-48 inches is the *distance* of maximum attacker effectiveness. The *area* of maximum attacker effectiveness is the distance plus a lateral area (width) extending about 10-15 degrees to the left or right from the direct line of attack at most. *(See Figure 2.)* Keep in mind that if the attacker turns to the left or right the area shown will also move with his line of sight and resultant body movement.

The worst place for a defender to be —or remain—is in the attacker's area of

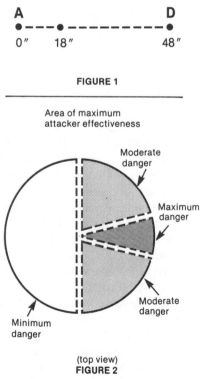

A ● – – ● – – – – – – – – ● **D**

0″   18″   48″

FIGURE 1

Area of maximum
attacker effectiveness

Moderate
danger

Maximum
danger

Minimum
danger

Moderate
danger

(top view)
FIGURE 2

maximum effectiveness. To remain in this area is to court disaster. You must move out of this area or alter the direction of his attack (by blocking or deflecting the attack). Avoidance by the defender must be centered on the idea of avoiding personal injury.

Fortunately, as a defender you have more alternatives open to than does the attacker. He is committed to a course of action—you aren't! Your attacker usually has committed himself and his ki to a forward motion of some sort. His commitment is your greatest asset. Once sensed, you will know where he wants to go (direction) as he does. He's committed to some form of forward motion whether it's a straight punch, roundhouse, overhead club attack or a knife swipe. He's committed. It behooves you to move out of his way; to avoid being the target.

There are many directions you can move, especially when combined with direct or deflective blocks. (A *direct* or hard block seeks to *stop* the force of the attack. A *deflective* block seeks to *change the direction* of the force of the attack without eliminating or stopping the momentum of the attack.) Most blocks in jujitsu are deflective blocks. There are two reasons for this. First, deflective blocks do not require as much energy to work properly. Second, deflective blocks can redirect the force of the attack so that it (the force or attacker's ki) can be used by the jujitsian against his assailant. Blocks are generally used in conjunction with a variety of evasive moves even though sometimes it's just as easy to sidestep an attack and let it go past you before responding.

Avoidance maneuvers are quite simple in themselves. They can be combined with a variety of blocks depending upon your training, orientation in the art, and the situation. There are three general maneuvering strategies. First, you can move straight in toward the attacker or move straight back. *(See Figure 3.)* This approach must, by necessity, include a block to stop or deflect the force of the attack. Second, you may move laterally, to the right or the left of the direction of the attack. *(See Figure 4.)* Lateral moves may or may not include blocks, depending upon the attack. When moving laterally, it is always more effective to use

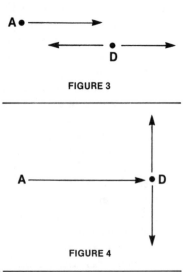

FIGURE 3

FIGURE 4

deflective blocks. As you're not moving in a direct line with the force of the attack, as in Figure 3, the use of a direct block combined with a lateral move is more difficult to execute effectively and may knock you off balance.

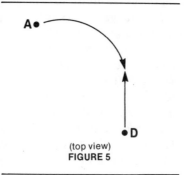

(top view)
FIGURE 5

What might appear as an exception to this rule are attacks delivered with a circular motion. Examples of this might be a roundhouse punch, knife swipe, or a lateral swing of a club. In this case your lateral motion should usually be combined with a direct block. In this type of situation the attack is still coming directly toward you. *(See Figure 5.)*

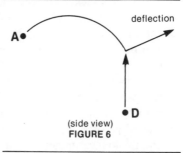

(side view)
FIGURE 6

Lastly, it is possible to move vertically, either up or down, to avoid the attack. In this case your block may either be of the direct or deflective type although it is usually a combination of the two. *(See Figure 6.)* As you are still possibly in the line of attack you must avoid becoming the target. However, for full protection the force of the attack must also be deflected.

Usually the three maneuvers are combined in one way or another. While not mentioning each maneuver here there are at least 32 different combinations of defensive maneuvers, not including blocks, that can be developed from the three basic maneuvers mentioned. Not all of the 32 different combinations can be used on all attacks. Some evasive maneuvers are more effective and realistic than others.

Your attacker has committed his ki toward one direction. You have 32 directions you can move and all you've done is removed yourself as a target. Would you like to go after a target that could do at least 32 different maneuvers to change its position? Those aren't good odds to go up against—and they get worse.

Removing yourself as a target is the first half of targeting the attacker. Unless you get out of the way of his attack you will really reduce your odds at being able to counter his attack. Targeting your attacker is the second half of the maneuvering strategy.

As your attacker's most effective range is 18-48 inches, so is yours if you plan to respond with a strike or kick. If you plan to throw your attacker using jujitsu techniques your effective range is 0-48 inches depending upon the attack he used, your evasive maneuver, and how you move into your attacker for targeting purposes. As a defender there are six horizontal and four vertical moves you can make in moving into your attacker so that you can execute a defensive technique. *(See Figures 7 and 8.)* In Figure 8 you may either kneel or drop to the right or left side of your attacker and respond from the front. You may also kneel or drop to the right or left side of the attacker and respond with your attack on either side.

The six horizontal and four vertical moves can be combined to form 24 different ways to move into your attacker. Admittedly some maneuvers, as some of the avoidance maneuvers, are more effective and realistic than others. With 32 potential evasive moves and 24 potential offensive moves you're not going to make a very good target. Usually an evasive move is combined with an offensive move. Do you want to guess how many potential and different maneuvers can be executed using these moves?

The evasive and offensive maneuvers have advantages and disadvantages. Moving into your attacker can prevent hits or kicks from being delivered effectively as well as set your attacker up for a large variety of throws, takedowns, or

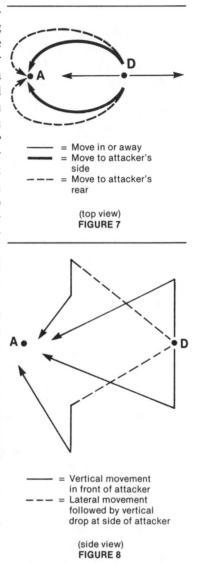

——— = Move in or away
▬▬▬ = Move to attacker's side
– – – = Move to attacker's rear

(top view)
FIGURE 7

——— = Vertical movement in front of attacker
– – – = Lateral movement followed by vertical drop at side of attacker

(side view)
FIGURE 8

come-alongs. Moving away from or out of the way of the attack can result in the attacker overextending himself and make techniques relying on ki easier to execute. Dropping down onto your knee or your side as an evasive move prior to moving in for a counter can be an effective surprise.

Unfortunately it also puts you on the ground.

Some maneuvers have more advantages than others. A few should be used only when no other alternatives are available. The situation will usually dictate what maneuvers you can make. Your knowldege and practice will determine what moves you are capable of making.

Jujitsu makes maximum use of the maneuvering strategies mentioned. Because jujitsu is such a flexible art, containing elements found in judo, aikido, and karatedo, a student effectively combining maneuvering strategies with jujitsu techniques can be a difficult foe to face. There is no way to predict what he will do, what way he will move, or what technique or techniques he will use when attacked. As a proficient jujitsu student can work from any angle and respond to his attacker from any direction it is extremely difficult to counter jujitsu techniques. Even if they are skilled jujitsian will have another technique to deal with the counter and *help* the attacker go in the direction he desires.

CHAPTER 3
Variations of Basic Techniques:
$1 + 1 =$ Infinity

Moving into your attacker for an effective counter is an important part in learning any martial art. If you can't get out of the way of the attack you won't be in any shape to effectively deal with your attacker. This book, as the first one, has a number of techniques designed to deal with a variety of attacks. You, the student, should realize that there are many variations of these jujitsu techniques and that many of them can be combined in a variety of ways. However, before you can effectively start coming up with viable variations and combinations you must *know* the art. You must know the techniques in terms of how and why they work the way they do.

Professor Jack Seki, my instructor for many years, always stressed what he called "knowing the art." He made the following three statements in various ways during my years of study under him:

1. If you don't *know* the techniques, they won't help you on the street. In a street situation, if you have to think of what moves you're going to make,

it's already too late. Reactions must be automatic.

2. Speed won't help you if you don't *know* the technique. Speed has a definite advantage on the street. However, a fast and sloppy technique has a lesser chance of succeeding than one done a bit slower but correctly. Of course combining quality and speed is even better, but I have never emphasized speed in my classes. I can't give my students speed. Once they really know a technique they can speed it up.

3. *Knowledge* gives you flexibility. This statement can be applied to any aspect of daily life, and it also applies to the martial arts. The more you *know* your art, the more flexible you can be. Techniques can be suited to the situation, and responses to attacks can be varied, giving you greater and more effective control over your opponent. If a technique doesn't work you can go into something else. If the situation changes you can change. Flexibility of this kind only comes with knowledge.

The problem is, knowing a martial art requires patience, repetition, understanding, experimentation, and evaluation. These five actions—or steps —are absolutely essential. This is also the order in which they must occur. One is an outgrowth of the other.

Patience
A person seriously studying a martial art must have patience. It takes many small steps to climb a mountain, and the steps must be in certain places. Learning is not a rapid do-it-once-know-it process. It requires being patient with yourself and allowing yourself to grow at your own rate.

Repetition
Repetition. To some people that's an awful word. "How many times do I have to repeat this move?" The best answer is probably, "forever." Repetition is that part of learning that sets the body movements down in your brain where they eventually will become automatic reactions. Only repetition can develop that.

Understanding
If you have a good instructor, one who explains why techniques work the way they do, you can develop a more complete understanding of the art. This is a critical element. If you don't understand how and why techniques work, you can never gain real insight into your art or make any substantial connections between its physical, theoretical, and philosophical aspects.

Not all instructors are capable or willing to give this information. Some feel explanation enhances learning. Others feel that allowing a student to "discover" the information through his own experience is more valuable. In either case acquiring an understanding of what you're doing is necessary if any real and continuous growth is going to take place.

Experimentation

Experimentation is a logical next step. You will take your knowledge and try to do things differently. It may be because you think there is a better way to do a technique. Whether or not you really find superior forms of various techniques is not as important at this stage as going through the process. Sometimes your ideas may not work out, and you will realize the tried-and-true method is best. Sometimes your instructor may learn something too.

Experimentation also allows you to put techniques together in different combinations. Some combinations will work extremely well, and others won't. Again the process is more important than the result. You will discover, hopefully with an instructor's support and guidance, that you can develop a system that works for you. The process also gives insight into your own abilities and limitations.

Evaluation

Perhaps the most difficult part of knowing an art is the ability to evaluate objectively. Does a particular technique work well for you? Are your modifications realistic and effective? Do they merely look good or do they really work? Can other practitioners make the same techniques work for them? Are the techniques you've learned simple and effective, or have you created a 27-move monster that has no real applicability?

Evaluating your acquisition of knowledge requires that you be honest with yourself. It requires that you be able to admit error to yourself and others. It means also that you must be willing to go back to step one and start over again if necessary.

The five steps (patience, repetition, understanding, experimentation and evaluation) form a circular or spiral pattern. One leads to the next, and the last (evaluation) brings you back to the first (patience). Knowing a martial art should be a continuous process, one that never ends.

Getting to Know Jujitsu

This five-step process is most evident in learning *jujitsu*, the "gentle art." Because of this, getting to *know* jujitsu is an art in itself. Jujitsu has served as the parent art from which judo, aikido, some forms of karate (especially kenpo), kendo, and other martial arts developed. However this explanation is like opening Pandora's box. Where does a jujitsu student start learning, and where does he stop?

There are perhaps 30 to 50 basic kata in jujitsu, not including hits, kicks, strikes, nerve attacks or pressure points.

In order to develop a better understanding of both the simplicity and the complexity of jujitsu, it is necessary to explain the difference between *kata* and *waza* in the art. A jujitsu kata is a specific form of throw, takedown, come-along hold, submission, and so on. A waza is a specific technique (series of moves) that may combine the basic forms along with hits, strikes, kicks, nerve attacks and modifications of basic forms. The basic kata do not include doing the basic forms from the left side, left-handed, reverse position (such as using a basic hip throw, *koshi nage*, to throw an opponent backward so he'll land face down) or modifications to the basic kata. The kata themselves are relatively simple; the combinations and variations are endless. Sounds like an impossible task to master—but it really isn't.

If you follow the five steps mentioned earlier, you can develop a logical sequence of meaningful learning. Through patience and repetition you will develop a feeling for forms and techniques, both of which are necessary to perfect the physical aspect of the art. If you have an instructor who can explain how and why techniques work, then you can develop understanding.

You will learn how techniques feel when they're executed properly. This knowledge will in turn help develop the necessary instinct to determine if techniques are working properly in a street situation. If a technique isn't working properly, you can change it without any conscious effort. You will also discover in throws where and how your attacker will land.

In doing this you will develop control. If you can sense that a technique is working properly, you are controlling your attacker. If you know how and where your attacker will end up after you're done with him, you are controlling your attacker.

Once these areas have been developed, a knowledgeable jujitsu student can, by the very nature of the art, begin experimenting. You will combine kata and rearrange waza to form a more *flexible* system suited to your own physical capabilities. Personalizing techniques is one of the major objectives in jujitsu as a means of self-defense.

This personalizing—or "knowing"—process can be overwhelming in itself because of the infinite number of juitsu combinations and variations. There is always the danger that you will become so engrossed in finding *new* combinations that you will lose contact with the basics which gave you the knowledge and flexibility to discover the combinations and variations. There is the danger that you may become so specialized that the original "system" is no longer a part of your practical knowledge.

To cope with such a problem, it is always good to remember the five steps of learning. As you progress with your instructor's help, combining techniques and reordering sequences, there is an occasional feeling of excitement and accomplishment when you enthusiastically call your teacher to your side and say, "Gee Sensei, I just made up a *new* technique!"

Is it possible for students to come up with new techniques? In some rigid martial arts it may not be possible. Jujitsu however is an open and flexible art. A new technique is quite possible.

There are two reasons why new techniques in jujitsu are possible. First, if you have a good *knowledge* of the basic forms, it is quite possible for you to discover new combinations in the process of experimenting. Secondly, even though there may be only 30 to 50 kata in the art, the combinations and variations are endless. Jujitsu is an endless art. Basic jujitsu kata are designed to be integrated with one another in a variety of ways; therefore, it is possible to move from one basic form into another. You can combine basic forms to create different techniques. Lastly, you may add modifications to the basic moves (based upon learned skills) and include nerve attacks, pressure points, hits, strikes. Simple and yet complex.

Two examples of this process are shown here. You would start out with a basic drop throw (*tai otoshi, See Table I*) and move into a one-knee drop throw to counter resistance or make the throw more effective. The basic

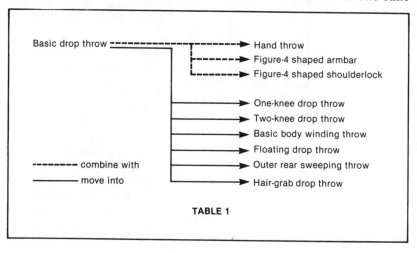

TABLE 1

drop throw could also be combined with a basic hand throw *(te nage)*.

The basic hand throw *(te nage, See Table 2)* could be changed to a wristlock takedown which could then be altered into an outside winding takedown. It might also be able to add a shoulder- or elbow-strike takedown or hair-grab come-along to the wristlock takedown.

When techniques are combined there is always a chance the resulting technique may be greater than the sum of its parts. The basic drop throw sequence *(See Table 1)* provides and excellent example. A basic hand throw is designed to apply pressure on the wrist so the attacker will have a "choice" of either being thrown or having his wrist snapped and be thrown. A body-drop throw is designed to throw the attacker by putting him off balance while leaning forward and then tripping his leg out from under him. By combining the two techniques it might appear there are two areas used to execute the throw: the opponent's wrist and his right lower leg.

Wrong. There are now *three* specific areas where pressure is applied quickly and effectively to execute the throw. In addition to the wrist and lower-leg action, effective pressure is also applied to the attacker's right elbow. How is this accomplished? Assuming that you're executing the hand throw and the drop throw properly, your body will be in a position where

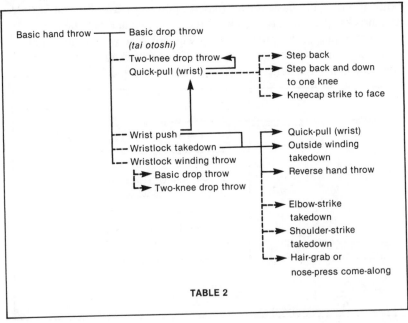

TABLE 2

the attacker's elbow is braced against your hip or upper right thigh. As you snap your right leg to execute the drop throw, while at the same time pressing and turning his hand, your body turns to your left thus applying pressure on the attacker's right elbow (which has been locked into its position by a combination of two techniques). Not only can you snap your opponent's wrist, you can also dislocate his elbow in the process of executing the throw. Damage done to the attacker as he hits the ground is not considered here; additional injuries could also take place on impact.

A further example is the idea of using a technique, normally taught for one type of attack (in this case a choke on the ground), and applying it to an entirely different type of attack. Combinations and variations of the technique are shown at the same time.

The sequence in *Table 3* is also useful in that it illustrates another one of the unique aspects of jujitsu. At times there are certain techniques, or combinations of techniques, which cannot be completed even in practice since injury is inevitable and unavoidable. If the cross-lapel armbar was set and the *tori* (defender) executed a body winding throw *(makikomi)* on his *uki* (attacker), a dislocated elbow and serious throat/neck injury to the uki would be unavoidable. Another example of such a situation would be a figure-4 shaped armbar *(ude guruma makikomi)* combined with an outside

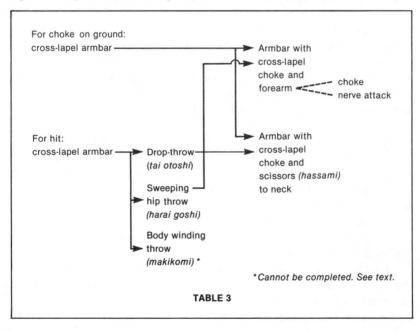

TABLE 3

33

sweeping winding throw *(harai makikomi).* This is a good reason for exercising extreme caution when experimenting and why complete knowledge of the techniques is *absolutely* necessary.

This concept can be applied to any form or kata in jujitsu.

The tables illustrate relative simplicity; only two to three possible steps were shown. It is quite possible to extend the process several steps, depending on the practitioner and his knowledge of the art. A good working knowledge of kata and waza is required to progress to this level of the art. With the knowledge and understanding of the forms and techniques in jujitsu, the roads are many and endless.

Accordingly, this is what makes jujitsu such a simple and yet complete art to learn: It is based upon the knowledge of the basic kata, as well as the integration with the other elements that make up the art. This comprises the basic foundation of the art—the primary knowledge from which growth can take place.

But the art is also exceedingly complex. As you develop an understanding of how and why the forms and techniques work, you can progress to the stage of moving from one technique into another or combining moves for the sake of either creating new combinations or refining ones already learned. It is then also possible to perfect a personalized system of self-defense.

As you deal with the complexity of the art, you are also faced with a storage/recall problem. My instructor would demonstrate a technique, then turn to me and say, "Did you get that down, Georgie?" "Hai!" I would say. He knew what I was doing. He always advised the serious student to write down techniques that were taught because he realized that it was impossible to remember them all. Those students of his who are still successfully teaching are so because they took his advice seriously.

You can log each variation or combination as a separate technique, as I have done and still do, if it turns out to be effective. There is no way to remember all of the variations; therefore, an effective recording and recall system must be developed (i.e., numbered index cards with key information on each technique). The other extreme is to look at the art in its simplicity, realizing that the combinations are endless. If the basic kata, waza, and so forth are known, then there may not be a need to have as formal of a recording and recall system.

In reality a middle course is usually chosen. This allows you to combine the assets of both positions. A knowledge of the techniques creates a potential for growth. Recording viable techniques, taught to you directly or developed from your knowledge, establishes a means by which you can pass on your knowledge. It also eventually means, as you understand the simplicty of the art, you can effectively deal with its complexities.

These three items (simplicity, complexity and the mental storage aspect) make jujitsu a continuous learning experience. This is why jujitsu is probably more difficult to master than other martial arts. In addition to perfecting already learned basic forms and techniques, there is the inherent challenge to modify and refine techniques, without withdrawing from the basic forms and techniques that led to the refinement. Also there is an eventual recognition, as illustrated in the figures, that the accumulated knowledge becomes geometric in proportion (1,2,4,8,16,32 etc.) in jujitsu rather than arithmetic (1,2,3,4,5, etc.) as in most other martial arts. In jujitsu the practitioner is always a student of the art, regardless of rank. There is not a point at which the acquisition of *knowledge* stops.

To be successful at any martial art you must *know* it. Just to be able to execute lightning-fast moves does not mean that you have mastered the art, it merely means that you're well-coordinated. To know a martial art you must have the patience to learn, sufficient practice and repetition to develop moves into automatic reactions, understanding of what you're doing as well as how and why it works, the knowledge to experiment, and the ability to objectively evaluate your growth within the art. This is a tall order though it can be accomplished.

To know jujitsu is to open the door to endless knowledge and growth. There is a concept in jujitsu called the circle theory. The five steps (patience, repetition, understanding, experimentation and evaluation) can form a continuous circular or spiral motion which never ends. Once the kata and waza are learned *and* understood, the road to growth is endless, dependent only upon the five actions and the jujitsuka's desire to continue growing. Jujitsu is as simple as it is complex. You can either develop its simplicity or complexity—or both. A successful student of jujitsu will learn the art—not just study it. He will understand it, and this goes far beyond the physical aspects of the art.

1 + 1 = infinity in jujitsu; growth is geometric and continuous. You can spend a whole life mastering the art and yet not have a complete grasp of every move or technique. It's what you do with the *knowledge* that counts. How do you deal with the questions from others when they ask what you're doing? You deal with it positively. The explanation may be long but, if you're a serious student of the art, it will be adequate and explain the method of your "madness."

"How many times do I have to do this technique?"

"Forever."

1

VARIATIONS OF THE BASIC DROP THROW

Basic Tai Otoshi

In the basic tai otoshi, as the attacker attempts to strike (1) the defender reaches under his foe's arm and (2) seizes his gi with both arms while moving his left leg in front of his right to prepare for a subsequent

2

3

move. (3) The defender then pivots in, placing his right leg in front of the opponent's. As the defender snaps his right leg into the attacker's right to begin the momentum, (4) he throws the attacker to the ground.

4

Tai Otoshi with Wristlock

The basic tai otoshi is now altered with the addition of a wristlock. (1) Grabbing and (2) twisting the wrist, (3) the defender steps across again and pivots. With the wrist still locked, (4) the defender gains momemtum from both the wristlock and the tai otoshi and (5) hurls his opponent to the ground. With the basic kata learned, students can try experimentation and thus add to the many variations.

2

4

5

Tai Otoshi with Armbar

In tai otoshi with an armbar variation,
(1) the root moves of attack and (2) subsequent hold by the defender are changed. The defender executes an armbar.
Additionally, (3) the defender holds the
attacker's right shoulder to allow room
for the pivot. Yet again, with the attacker restricted, the defender (4) leg
blocks, snaps and (5) throws. With so
many combinations, the student may
steer toward one that suits him best.

2

4

5

41

Tai Otoshi with Elbowlock

In the tai otoshi with the added elbow lock, the defender (1) blocks high the attacker's assault and (2) controls the attacker's arm with his lower arms rather than his hands. (3) The attacker pivots again but this time more to the attacker's hip. (4) Again blocking and snapping with his leg, (5) the defender brings the attacker to the ground.

2

4

5

43

Tai Otoshi
Dropping to One Knee

Now the legs are used in variations from tai otoshi with one knee. From a different angle one can see (1) the block, (2) sidestep, and (3) the pivot, leg block and snap. However, as the defender throws his opponent he (4&5) falls to one knee, greatly increasing the momentum of the throw rather than remaining on both feet. Personalizing techniques is one of the major objectives in jujitsu as a means of self-defense.

2

4

5

Tai Otoshi
Dropping to Both Knees

Further variations are seen with tai otoshi falling to both knees. Again (1) starting with the grab and subsequent step, (2) the defender pivots in and blocks with the leg. However, utilizing one of the many options available in jujitsu, rather than snapping the leg, (3) the defender simply drops to both knees (4&5), thus altering the center of gravity for the subsequent throw.

2

4

5

Tai Otoshi with Hair Grab

Here tai otoshi is amended with a hair grab. With (1) the grab, side step and (2) leg block completed, (3) the defender reaches around and grabs the attacker's hair. (4) Pulling his head down, (5) he snaps and throws. Note how tai otoshi is altered, providing countless new techniques from the same basic throw.

1

3

2

4

5

Tai Otoshi
with Floating Drop Throw

Illustrated is tai otoshi with a floating drop throw termination. The sequence (1) starts with the block, (2) stepping across with the left foot, (3) pivoting and block-

ing the opponent's leg. However, (4) the defender now throws his body to his right, and with a winding momentum, (5) brings the attacker to the floor.

VARIATIONS OF THE BASIC HAND THROW

Basic Tae Nage

(1) The defender is faced by the knife-wielding attacker. As the attacker (2) lunges in with the knife, the defender pivots and (3) grabs the wrist. He then (4) pivots back and adds his other hand to the grip. (5) The defender then pivots back again and starts turning the attacker's wrist. Because of the unnatural direction in which the attacker is forced, the defender is able to (6) throw him and (7) gain complete control.

Tae Nage and Step Back

(1) Starting with the confrontation (2), grab (3) and control of the basic hand throw. (4) Rather than pulling the attacker's wrist in front of him, the defender steps back on his right leg while

beginning the quick pull. (5) As the defender goes down on one knee, the attacker is completely under control so that the defender may (6) secure the weapon.

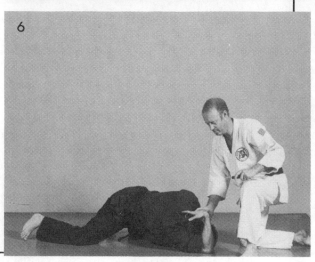

Tae Nage with Quick Pull and Wristlock Takedown

(1) The defender faces his assailant who holds the knife. (2) As the assailant lunges, the defender pivots and grabs the knife hand. (3) Pivoting back with the wristlock, the defender (4) executes a wrist pull to disoreint the attacker. (5) He pivots 180 degrees into the attacker and (6) lifts one leg to begin his drop. (7) Falling to his behind, he (8) rolls back slightly and gains control.

Tae Nage with Quick Pull and Kneecap Strike to Face

This sequence is interesting in that the defender has added two techniques in the middle of the basic hand throw. (1) As the attacker faces the defender, and (2) lunges. The defender avoids the stab, grabs the knife hand, and (3) executes the wristlock. (4) The defender executes a wrist pull (5) to bring the attacker to a crouch. He then (6) strikes with the knee to the attacker's face and (7) drops his leg to block the attacker's leg, and (8) executes the hand throw, maintaining pressure on the wrist (9) to gain control.

CHAPTER 4
Dealing with Multiple Attackers

I t's Saturday night and you're walking home alone. Suddenly, out of the darkness, you're confronted by two thugs. You try to talk your way out of the situation, but a physical confrontation appears inevitable.

Now's the time to apply all your martial arts training to a real-life situation. However, you've got *two* attackers, not one. What do you do? What factors should you consider? What strategies can you follow?

Most martial arts training is limited to the dojo, where situations are one-on-one; you have one attacker whom you are familiar with. Usually the attack is known—either a simulated street attack or a specific strike or kick.

Dealing with a single attacker is an excellent way to learn techniques and perfect them. Working freestyle with one attacker is an excellent way to develop speed, coordination, and techniques specifically suited to your abilities. One attacker allows you to deliver quick reactions and make simple decisions.

Two or more attackers are a whole different show. Most training doesn't deal with multiple attackers at all because of the complexities involved. It is not as simple and neat as working with a single assailant.

Techniques that work well in a single-attacker situation may be suicidal with two or more attackers. Split-second decisions must be made that cannot be anticipated and an instructor cannot forewarn you about. Unless carefully supervised, multiple-attacker situations can result in confusion, frustration and serious injuries.

However *not* dealing with the issue as part of the advanced student's training doesn't solve any problems either. Sweeping the matter under the rug by saying, "It's like dealing with two single attackers," oversimplifies the problem. Confronting the problem at least recognizes it and provides you with the opportunity of developing skills in that area. It at least gives you some experience even though it is in the controlled environment of a dojo.

Making the Best of a Bad Situation

A multiple-attacker confrontation is a bad street situation. It places a severe strain on strategy and skills. It requires flexibility in thinking. It also requires a much greater awareness of your immediate environment. It's never a simple matter, in other words. However, there are ways to make the best out of a bad situation.

There are four areas that should be considered. Three can be considered external factors (coming from outside of your body), and one an internal factor (coming from within your body). While this chapter cannot cover every aspect of multiple attackers, the four general areas it will consider are: (1) your environment or surroundings; (2) the concept of the circle; (3) the attackers, (these three are external factors); and (4) some basic strategies.

Environment and the Circle

Two of the external factors can be considered together, environment and the concept of the circle or wheel, as they're closely related. Your environment is everything around you in your immediate vicinity. The concept of the circle or wheel is usually referred to in most soft martial arts as the theory behind the continuous motion of the attacker and the utilization of his own ki to bring him down. This is an oversimplification of the circle theory, but is satisfactory for a brief explanation.

In dealing with multiple attackers, the concept of the circle has a somewhat different meaning. Consider yourself the center of a circle (or hub of a wheel) and think of your attackers as the rim.

If you think in these terms you can establish what can be called a *danger zone*. The danger zone, simply put, is that area in which an attacker can inflict injury on you. The danger zone generally starts about 18 inches from you and extends to a distance of about four feet—an area from which hits and kicks can effectively make contact with you. Closer than 18 inches, you will probably be faced with holds. They usually don't require as fast a response time—unless the second opponent is also attacking or the assailant holding you has a weapon.

Within the danger zone, your chief asset is your vision. You will rely on direct and peripheral vision as a warning of the attack. You will also have a blind zone. Your direct vision will give you a clear, sharp view of about 90 degrees (one-fourth of a circle). Peripheral vision will extend your sight to 180 degrees (one-half circle) and sometimes beyond that, depending on available light movement, and your eye sensitivity.

Your peripheral vision will usually warn you of an attack and is extremely important with multiple attackers, when a wide range of vision is essential. By scanning, you can also increase your area of direct vision. Effective use of your peripheral vision will also reduce your blind zone. (The blind zone, by the way, is the area behind you that you can't see.) If you can't see an attack coming at you, you can't effectively defend against it. Protect and move your blind zone constantly so as to have a greater view of the rim.

Sound is another factor to be considered in the environment of your circle. Sound can be an asset or liability. It can be an asset if it provides you with a clue as to where the attack is coming from. But it can also be used by one attacker to distract you from the other(s). Your ability to scan is your best tool in differentiating between clues and distraction.

The last factor to be considered in the environment of the circle is physical objects. What kind of surface are you on? Are you near or against a wall? Is there a curb, telephone pole, fire hydrant, or other obstacle in the circle or immediate vicinity? Any object in your circle can be used by you—or against you. It all depends on what you know.

A wall, for example, can be an asset or liability. It can protect your blind area, but it can also prevent you from escaping or using some of your techniques. If you know how to use a wall as an object within your circle, it is an asset. If you don't, it can be your *worst* enemy, as it cuts your circle in half, and severely limits your movement.

Attackers

The third external element that should be considered is the attackers. How many are there? How big are they? Do they have weapons? Where are they located on the rim? What is their injury potential and what is yours? These questions should be considered in deciding what course of action you will take. All of these items are of equal importance.

The number of attackers will have a direct effect on your survivability. Dealing with two attackers is relatively simple when compared to three attackers. Each additional attacker beyond two has a greater negative effect on your ability to survive.

How big are your attackers? Obviously their size and stature will have an effect on what you do. You may be lucky and have the opportunity of choosing which attacker to deal with first. If one of the attackers has a weapon, he poses a substantially greater threat.

The location of the attackers on the rim also determines what you can do. If they're both in front of you it's obviously better than having one in front and one behind you. You must also consider if one attacker is closer to you than the other. The other factors mentioned, when combined with this, would also determine whether the closest attacker poses a greater threat than one further away.

Lastly, putting all of this together, you must consider two main things about your attackers: which one poses the greatest threat to you over-all, and which one can you defeat with the greatest ease (a relative term)?

Strategies

"Good grief" you're probably saying at this point. "How do I think of all these things and defend myself at the same time?" It seems like an impossible situation.

It's not as bad as it sounds. Sometimes you may have several seconds (which is a lot of time) to size up a situation. Most of the external factors can be evaluated and decided upon in one or two seconds. Sometimes there appears to be no time at all and you have to make what seem to be instantaneous decisions. But even this is possible if your mind is trained at what to look for.

There are a few basic rules you can follow that will not only simplify things, but will also improve your chances of coming out on top against two or more attackers.

1. Don't use any techniques that will put you on the ground. If you do anything that puts you on the ground, you're really reducing your chances. If you're knocked to the ground, that's another story. You may have to defend yourself from there. (Do you know any ground defenses?) Don't use pins or ground submissions. They're effective with one attacker, but you're putting yourself in a bad position if the other attacker is still standing.

2. Use one attacker against the other whenever possible. Examples of this might be throwing one attacker into another, maneuvering them so they're in each other's way, or putting one attacker into a standing-submission or come-along hold so that he can be used as a shield against the other attacker(s). Throwing one attacker into another has the obvious advantage of "killing two birds with one stone"—creating confusion and fear among the attackers. In addition to any physical damage done.

Using one attacker as a shield also has physical and psychological benefits. If one attacker can be used as a shield, the others will have to get through him to get to you. Second, if the shield is being held with a *proper* hold you can create a lot of pain and injure him quite easily. (A proper hold is one in which the attacker's resistance or the final execution of the hold can result in a fracture and/or joint dislocation.) Both techniques can be used to prevent further assault upon you. If the other assailants see that their cohort is going to be the target of their attacks, or that you're in a position to inflict serious injury (as evidenced by the shield's cries of pain), they may recognize that you have control of the situation and retreat. If this occurs, continue to use the shield until you can safely remove yourself from the conflict.

3. Injure your first attacker as severely as possible. This is an extension of the second strategy, but its intent is serious bodily injury. The first attacker you deal with, according to the strategy, should not be able to get up or continue as an attacker, verbally or physically. The sole purpose of this stategy is to create enough pain in one attacker so that the others will be too scared to continue the assault. Your intent here is to create fear. This must be quick and devastating. It must make the other attackers think twice. It must create doubt in their minds about their chances of winning—and about the possiblity of being similarly injured.

While this strategy is an extension of *2*, it also reflects a basic difference in strategic choices. With *2*, you are attempting to get out of the situation by using the least force necessary. With *3*, it has become necessary to inflict serious injury to get your point across. Both strategies are directed toward accomplishing the same thing: getting out of the confrontation, but only having to deal directly with one attacker. Strategy *2* can quickly become *3* if the need arises. Your training and situation will determine which route you take.

4. Be aware of and use the danger-zone concept. Try to keep at least four feet between you and your attackers if possible. If closer contact is inevitable, you must be ready and able to use whatever techniques possible to bring your opponents down. This includes hits and kicks (to keep attackers further away or bring them down), as well as the use of nerves, pressure points, come-along skills, or throws, if your training is oriented toward close-in situations. Don't put yourself in a position where you can be hit, kicked, or grabbed if you can avoid it.

In using the danger-zone concept, you should have as large a repertoire of techniques as possible. Each martial art has limitations in the area of the circle. You should be aware of the limitations of your particular art and compensate for them. Generally speaking, the hits and kicks of most styles of karate are ineffective when the opponent is closer than 18 inches. Many aikido techniques are unusable if the opponent is too far away. Judo throws are usually effective only if solid body contact can be made. These generalizations are useful to illustrate the necessity of a wide repertoire, not one strictly limited to one art.

5. *Use eye contact and body language effectively.* The effective use of eye contact goes hand-in-hand with the danger-zone concept. With one attacker, you may be able to stare him down, causing him to back out of the situation. Appearing calm is also work in a multiple-attacker situation of the physical attack hasn't commenced yet, or if one attacker is down and the others are pausing for a moment. It is probably far more effective to maintain general eye contact with whoever seems to be the leader, while using your scanning ability to enhance your peripheral vision. Be careful though. A lot of eye movement and moving around quickly may be perceived (somewhat correctly) as fear. This may enhance your attacker's feelings of confidence.

6. *Be flexible!* This is the most important rule to follow. There are exceptions to all of the rules mentioned. Don't assume these strategies are rigid and absolute. They're not! They're simply good guidelines to improve your chances of survival.

Putting Strategies to Use

These strategies can be used to help you establish better control of a multiple-attacker situation. For example, if you have one attacker in front of you and one behind, remember the concept of the wheel. Step to one side or the other, thus moving the hub. Your attackers are still on the rim but you'll have a better view of them. If attack is imminent and you feel that you can get control of one attacker, do it and use him as a shield. If one attacker is holding you from behind and the person in front of you hasn't done anything yet, use strategy 2 or 3 (shield or severe injury) to take care of the person holding you. If the forward attacker is hitting you or has a weapon, you may have to ward him off with kicks, quickly deal with the rear attacker, and then continue with the forward foe. Be flexible in your thinking.

Conclusions

Dealing with multiple attackers is never a good situation. It demands all of your skills, knowledge, training, and a great deal of flexibility. If you can adapt the basic strategies presented here to your particular martial art, then your chances of success on the street can be improved.

You must be realistic. The more attackers you face at one time, the less your chances are of winning. What you see in "socky-chop" movies may look good, but life doesn't work that way—neither does the street. As in any street situation, whether it be against one or more attackers, *you must establish control* of the situation. With one attacker, you may not have to inflict any actual physical injury. Chances are, the fight will be much more serious if you are attacked by more than one. If you must injure an assailant, make sure it looks and sounds bad enough to cause the other attacker(s) to think twice.

Keep control of yourself and control of the situation. This is the primary rule in any situation in which you hope to succeed, whether in your daily life or in a street confrontation. If you have control, or even limited control of the situation, you have better control of the outcome. If you lose control of yourself, it's guaranteed that you'll lose control of the outcome.

Success on the street is determined by good training in the dojo. Work with multiple attackers in a variety of situations. If you have a VCR setup, use it. It's the best tool for viewing what happened, what worked, and what didn't. Rely on your instructor for pointers on how to survive multiple attackers. He may spot things you don't, both good and bad. Be aware, however, that some multiple-attacker defenses cannot be fully executed at normal speed when practicing (such as throwing one attacker into another or into a wall). Great care and self-control must be demonstrated out of respect to your partners.

Most street situations can be prevented or avoided. Some cannot. Multiple attackers *are* a bad situation. But with proper training, you can make the best of a bad situation and hopefully come out the victor.

AGAINST MULTIPLE ATTACKS

Grabbed from Behind

(1) Walking through a park, the defender (2) is suddenly grabbed from behind while another assailant (3) confronts him with a knife. The knife-wielding opponent is more dangerous, so the defender (4) disarms him with a kick, (5) initiating a spinning move against the second attacker. This move is critical, for he must successfully escape the grab in order to (6) reverse the hold (6A) with an armbar, and (7) use one attacker as a shield against the other.

2

4

5

7

Both Attackers within the Danger Zone

(1) Both attackers are within the defender's danger zone. The defender (2) strikes quickly to (3) disable the first opponent in time to (4) ward off the second by blocking his strike. (5) Stepping in and pivoting into the second opponent, the defender keeps the first opponent in his peripheral vision. (6) Seeing the first opponent recover to his feet, the defender (7) throws the second opponent toward the first, (8) inhibiting his advance, and the defender (9) steps back in a safe direction.

Against a Wall

Here, the defender (1) is trapped, and one attacker is armed with a piece of broken glass. The defender (2) uses the wall in his favor, countering the attacker's grasp by (3) executing an

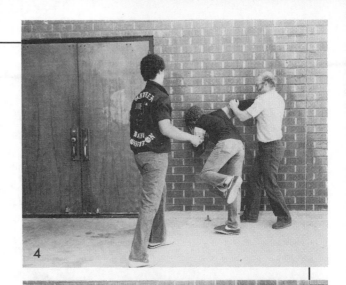

armlock, and (4) smashing him head first into the wall. Then, (5) grabbing his hair, he (6) uses him as a shield against the attacker armed with the broken glass.

CHAPTER 5

What Constitutes
a Complete Jujitsu Technique

T he terms *kata* and *waza* received only cursory attention in the glossary of *Jujitsu: Basic Techniques of the Gentle Art*. In that book, kata was simply referred to as *form* and waza was referred to as a *technique*. This may have resulted in some confusion, especially when the phrase *jujitsu technique* or simply *technique* was used elsewhere in either my first book or this one. Some additional explanation is needed to clear up any confusion.

A *jujitsu technique* or *technique* can refer to any kata *or* waza in the art. In that context, it is a general term that should be used as such. Technique does not refer only to *waza* except in the promotional examinations. In fact, *technique* can even refer to the actual execution of a kata or waza, referring to the manner in which that kata or waza is executed.

Kata and waza do have more extensive definitions. To leave the reader with the simple definitions previously given would be a gross injustice to the art and to the intermediate student, who needs a more complete explanation. In jujitsu, a kata is a specific form, such as a hip throw, nerve attack, submission, etc. A kata is a specific form within a waza. The number of kata in jujitsu is almost infinite when one adds variations.

When examining a student in the kata portion of a promotional examination, the examiner looks at how well and accurately the specified kata is performed even though it may be mixed with other kata. For example, if a student is asked to execute an *ippon seol nage* (one-arm hip throw) on the brown belt test, he may actually start with a *te no tatake* (block), go to a *te tatake* (striking technique), execute the ippon seol nage, and finish off with an *ude guruma* (armbar) submission. While all of these would enhance the performance and indicate a complete waza, the examiner would still base his score mainly on the actual kata requested. The reason for the concentration on kata—or form—is that the technique must be done properly in order to be effective. Kata emphasizes the *art* of the technique.

A *waza*, on the other hand, is a combination of moves, or kata. A complete waza has the following elements: 1) a response to the attack, such as a block for a hit; 2) a follow-through, such as a throw, nerve attack, takedown, etc.; and 3) a submission, such as a pin, strike, come-along, or standing or ground submission.

In the waza portion of the examination, the examiner would be looking at the *effectiveness* of the technique as well as its completeness. The student would be judged on the technique used, its application to the specific situation, and the various parts that make up a complete waza. The examiner should be aware that a complete waza may not be executed for every attack. The examiner should be looking at the student's ability to react quickly, automatically, and effectively to the attacks.

Having presented a more complete definition and comparison of kata and waza in jujitsu, there is only one more term that needs a more adequate definition: a *complete* jujitsu technique. What is a complete jujitsu technique? First, it has all of the elements of a complete waza; a response, a follow-through, and a submission. In addition, a complete jujitsu technique usually has elements in it that can be more specifically found in the three *do* or ways that have evolved from jujitsu.

A complete jujitsu technique may use elements of judo (*ju* = gentle, *do* = way—gentle way) in the form of throws, use of leverage, pins, hold downs and chokes. It may use elements that make up aikido (*ai* = mind, *ki* = spirit, *do* = way—way of mind and spirit), in the form of the use of nerves, attacker ki, joint locks, and holds. A complete technique may use elements of karatedo (*kara* = empty, *te* = hand, *do* = way—way of the empty hand), in which strikes, hits, and kicks are used.

It is very common for aikido or karatedo moves to start or end a technique with moves from judo in between. Of course, it's also possible for a technique to contain only one or two of the three *do* that make a complete jujitsu technique. The three *do* can also be in any order and may be repeated as called for. Just because a jujitsu technique does not have all three *do* in it, that does not mean that it isn't effective. Jujitsu techniques are effective. It just is not a complete jujitsu technique if one looks at the art in a very rigid manner.

In this book I will try to present complete jujitsu techniques as much as possible, as I did in my first book. There are advantages and disadvantages to this type of format. On the plus side, showing complete techniques immediately shows the student how moves are put together and how one flows into the next. Rather than dealing with specific movements, as in kata exercises, the student immediately applies his knowledge to a street-type attack. By learning it all together he can see how it should work. If jujitsu techniques are *taught* as complete techniques, that's how they should be shown and practiced. As a student develops proficiency in the execution of complete jujitsu techniques it is much easier for him to develop variations at any stage of execution.

On the negative side, as the specific moves and kata are not shown seperately, as in most *do*, they may be initially more difficult to learn. This is the only disadvantage. The advantages have more strengths than the disadvantages. The student will learn faster in the long run, and he will have a more effective repertoire of techniques to draw from.

CHAPTER 6

Intermediate Techniques

The techniques presented in this section are designed to round out your basic technical knowledge of the art with respect to the brown belt examination (which also serves as a basis for the black belt performance examination). In this section, you will be concerned with attacks that can be made against you while you are in a standing position. In addition to the techniques presented, additional loosening up moves and submission techniques are also shown to help you develop *complete* jujitsu techniques as described earlier in the text.

These 35 techniques are also cross-referenced with a variety of different attacks as shown on the Technique/Attacks Cross Reference Chart. As in the first book, these are all core techniques, basic to the understanding of the mechanics of the art. Once you have mastered the technique as shown in the book, feel free to develop variations to suit the additional attacks listed on the chart for each technique.

INTERMEDIATE TECHNIQUES

Shoulder Grab Rear Throw
(Ura Nage)

(1) From a ready position (tachi waza), (2) as your opponent swings at you, deflect the blow to your right with your left hand. Step forward with your left foot as you block. (3) Step behind the opponent with your right foot. Your right hand grabs his left shoulder from underneath your left arm with your right palm down. Grab the opponent's right shoulder with your left hand, palm down. (4) Step across with your right leg behind his legs. Pivot on the balls of your feet so your feet are pointed almost to your left. (5) Drop to your right knee, pulling your opponent over your shoulder, as you turn to your left. (As he goes over, pull your partner towards you to prevent him from striking the mat with his head. He won't see the mat until it's in front of him.) Your right kneecap should come down just behind his left heel if possible. (6) Keep hold of your opponent. (7) Pull the opponent up with both of your hands and (8) turn him over, bringing your left arm down over his head. Bring his head up so that the base of his skull rests on your left thigh. Pull back with your left hand to execute the choke. (9) If your opponent manages to balance himself by resting on his elbow, as in the previous step, bring your left foot in front of his forearm and slide your foot back, thus unbalancing him, and effecting a more secure hold.

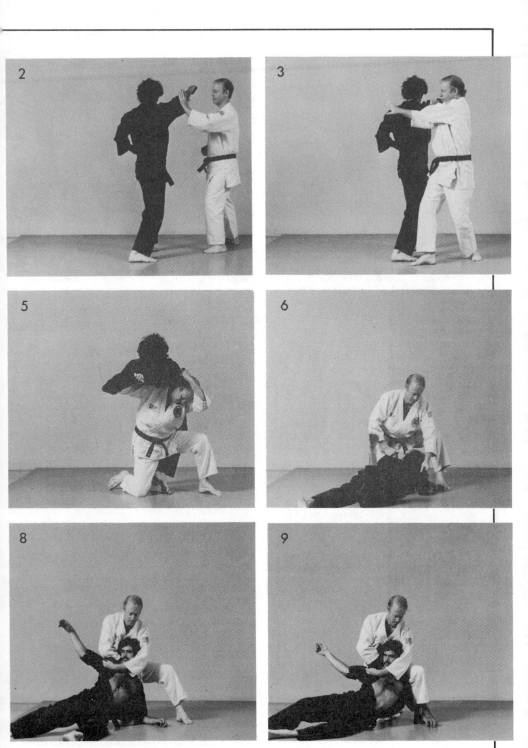

Elbow Rear Throw
(Ushiro Hiji Nage)

(1) Assume a ready position for a straight knife thrust. (2) Pivot your right foot back clockwise, thus getting your body out of the way of the knife thrust. (3) Your right hand grabs the back of the opponent's knife hand, and pushes it away as your right foot steps back in. (3A) Note that your thumb and last two digits are around the attacker's wrist. (4) As you continue to push the knife hand away, grab the attacker's sleeve with your left hand, and pull it as your left foot slides back in a counterclockwise direction. (5) Continue this circular motion, bringing the knife up toward the opponent and (6) executing the throw. (7) Go down onto your right knee as the throw is completed. (8) To finish the technique, bring the knife against the attacker's throat and (9) slice by pulling up on his hand. The hand hold, as shown in the previous insert, should be maintained during the entire technique.

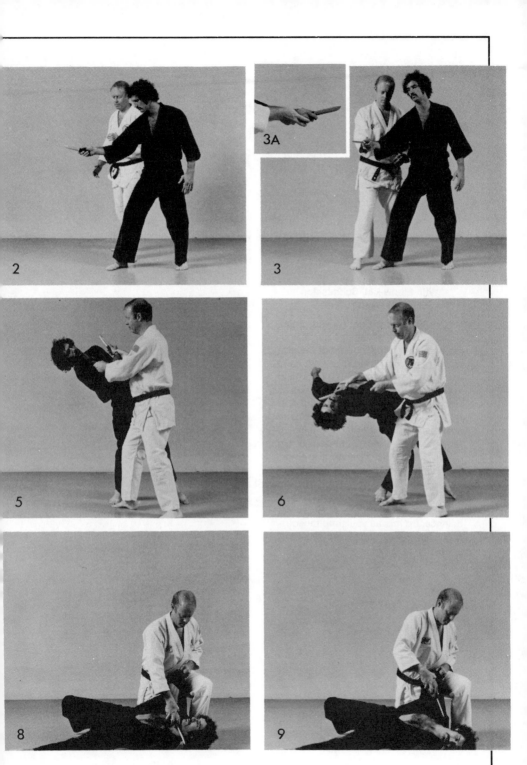

3A

2

3

5

6

8

9

Double-Strike Turning Throw
(Ude No Tatake)
With Elbow-Roll Submission
(Hiji Tatake Shimi Waza)

(1) In a ready position, (2) your opponent grabs both of your lapels. (3) Your left hand grabs your opponent's sleeve above his elbow. Bring your right hand up and across so you can (4) backhand your opponent in his right lower ribs as a distraction. (5) Step forward with your right foot as you bring your right arm up in between his arms. You should be facing to your left at this time. (6) Strike outward on your opponent's elbow with your right hand. The outward strike is initiated with your forearm perpendicular to the ground. The strike is designed to put the attacker off balance. Do this as you simultaneously pull his sleeve, and (7) pivot your left

2

4

5

7

Continued

8

foot back, (8) causing the attacker to fall. Go down onto your right knee, (9) keeping hold of the attacker as shown. (10) For the elbow-roll submission (elbow roll-hiji tatake shimi waza), your right hand comes up and grabs the back of his hand as shown, with your thumb in between his thumb and index finger. Do not grab his wrist. (11) Your left hand cups slightly (sara) so that his elbow is resting in your palm. (12) Continue turning his wrist and rolling his elbow (13) to bring the attacker down (14) onto his stomach. (15) Elbow-roll submission is complete at this point. If you wish you may rest or drop your left kneecap onto his elbow as an alternative.

10

13

Multiple Strike Belt Throw (Obi Nage) With Forearm-Roll Choke (Shimi Waza)

(1) From a ready position, (2) your attacker attempts to strike with his right fist. Block it to your left with your left forearm. (3) Strike the opponent under his chin with your right forearm as you step in with your right foot. Keep hold of the attacker's right arm with your left hand. (4) Your right forearm slides off of his chin. Bring it around in front of you as you

turn to your left. Keep a tight hold of his arm or sleeve with your left hand. Your right hand should be in a semi-closed fist with your palm facing you. (5) Strike back at your opponent's head with your elbow, hitting him just below the ear. Keep his right arm pulled tight for maximum impact. (6) Bring your right arm up,

Continued

and (7) around the opponent's neck. (7A) Except in an actual fight, you should always rest your right hand, palm up, on your partner's chest so he can tuck his head as he's thrown and avoid injury. (7B) In an actual self-defense situation, wrap your arm completely around the attacker's neck. Holding the attacker in this manner would cause his head to strike the ground as he is thrown. Grab your opponent's belt from behind with your left hand, palm down, facing his back. (8) Bring your opponent toward

10

you, and start to go down as your right foot blocks his right foot. (9) Go down, pulling your opponent over you. (10) As he goes over, your right foot assists in the throw by lifting his right leg up and over at his instep. (11) Once your opponent is thrown, your left hand lets go of his belt, and clamps onto your right wrist to choke the opponent. (12) Roll your opponent over onto his face with your body over his head and your feet apart for balance, to finish the technique.

11

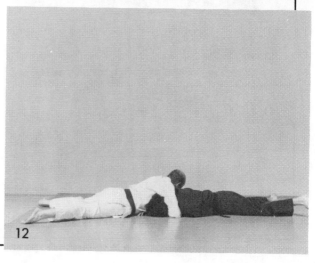

12

Floating Drop Throw (Uki Otoshi)

(1) Assume a ready position, (2) as your opponent attempts to strike, block his punch away, stepping in with your left foot at the same time. (3) As you move in toward the attacker, grab his right lapel with your

3

right hand. (4) Step in beyond the attacker with your right foot, causing the attacker to lose his balance, and/or push back against your body with his body. (5) As he pushes his body

4

5

Continued

6

against you, fall back (6) toward his left, pulling him toward your left. (7) This will cause him to fall to your left as you land on your left side (at about a 45-degree angle from the attacker). Be sure to keep your body straight as you fall. If you don't you'll land on your seat and

7

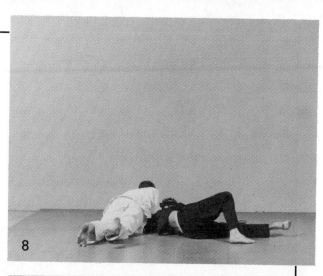

the throw won't work properly. (8) Once the opponent is down, turn your body to your left, rolling up his arm. (9) Lift his arm up, slide your right leg under it, and set a figure-4 armbar as shown. (10) Secure the armbar by putting your left leg over your right foot.

Foot-Twist Side Throw
(Ashi Yoko Nage)
With Figure-4 Leg Lock
(Ashi Guruma)

(1) Assume a ready position. (2) As your opponent attempts a front kick, deflect and hook the kick to your right by blocking out (with a closed hand) and then moving your right forearm up, opening your hand after the block is completed. (3) Reach over with your left hand, and grab the heel of your opponent's foot. (4) Grab at the ball of his foot with your right hand. (4A) Note that your right hand will act as the pivot point for this throw, serving as a socket as his heel serves as the ball. (5) Pivot your left foot back, as you (5A) turn the attacker's foot counterclockwise. (6) This movement will throw the attacker. (7) Once the opponent is down, you can

2

4

5

Continued

(8) go into a figure-4 leg lock (ashi guruma) submission by bringing your left foot forward as you keep hold of his right foot with both hands. (9) Keep the attacker's leg off the ground as you step over it with your right foot. (10) Bring your right foot down in between the attacker's legs. on the right side of your foot, with your toes toward the attacker's crotch. Bend his leg as you go down. (Go down very carefully in practice to avoid separating your attacker's knee joint.) (11) Once down, bring his right foot over to your right side. You may now let go of his foot with your hands. (His foot is put into this position so that you can keep all your weight to the left and forward of his foot. He thus cannot force you backwards by straightening out his leg.) (12) Bring your left foot up to the left side of the attacker's waist and lean forward to separate his kneecap. To enhance the hold as a pin, you can grab attacker's hair or the back of his gi with your left hand for extra support. (13) To get out of the submission roll to your right, (14) thus releasing the lock. (15) This is the *only* safe way to get out of this lock without risking serious injury to you or your partner. Do *not* stand up to release lock. You may lose your balance.

8

10

13

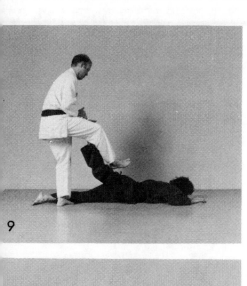

9

11

12

14

15

Leg Winding Throw
(Ashi Makikomi)
With Leglock Lift Submission
(Ashi Shimi Waza)

(1) Assume a ready position. (2) As your opponent attempts a kick, (3) block and deflect the kick as in the previous technique. (4) Hook his leg in your arm as you bring your right arm up and step forward with your right foot. (5) Bring your left hand up and grab onto the back of your right hand, holding his leg tight against you. Turn to your left to throw. (6) Be sure that you lean back slightly so his right foot can't come around and hit your head as he's thrown. (7) Go down onto your right knee as the throw is completed. Make sure his foot is lodged against your upper arm. (8) To execute the leglock lift submission (ashi shimi waza), turn your right forearm up and inwards toward your chest as it slides up his Achilles tendon.

2

4

5

7

8

1

2

Wrist Side Throw
(Haiai Nage
or Tekubi Yoko Nage)

(1) From a ready position, (2) your opponent grabs both your wrists. (3) Pull your left wrist back and forth (as a distraction), as you turn your right wrist out of his

3

grip by bringing it up (4) in a clockwise circle against his thumb. (5) Turn your left hand in a clockwise circle, coming around and up over

4

5

Continued

the back of his right hand. (6) Bring your right hand up to rest your right fingers against your extended left fingers (6A) at a right (90-degree) angle. (7) Continue turning your hands clockwise until your left palm is facing down and his hand is facing palm up. (8&9) Bring your opponent down by (10)

9

continuing downward pressure on his wrist. (11) Go down onto your right knee to finish the throw. Note: This technique must be done very quickly in order to work. Otherwise the attacker will be able to let go of your wrist. The next technique will assist you in case this happens.

10

11

Striking Technique (Te Tatake)

Use this option in case your opponent lets go of you in Step 6 of the previous technique. This is an example of flexibility. You should always have something else in mind in case your original technique doesn't work. (1) From a ready position, (2) your opponent

grabs both your wrists. (3) Pull your left wrist back and forth (as a distraction), as you turn your right wrist out of his grip by bringing it up (4) in a clockwise circle against his thumb. (5) Turn your left hand in a clockwise circle, coming around and over the back of his

Continued

6

7

right hand. (6) Bring your right hand up to rest your right fingers against your extended left fingers at a right angle. At this point, your opponent lets go of your wrist. (7) Continue the clockwise motion of your hands in a clockwise circle, (8) so that you end up next

8

to the opponent. (9) You then reverse your arm and body motion, turning counterclockwise to your left and striking your opponent in the chest with your left elbow. (10) Then strike your opponent under the chin or against his nose with a left backhand.

9

10

Side Winding Throw
(Yoko Makikomi)

This is the "art" version of the variation that follows. This version will work if perfected. The variation that follows is a "safe" version of this technique. (1) In a ready position, (2) the attacker grabs both wrists. This version if identical to the technique following this except that it relies on the attacker to keep hold of your wrist rather than you his. If the attacker's hold is strong and you move through the technique quickly and smoothly, it will work. (3) Bring the attacker's left arm down and his right arm up as your fingers point away from you and toward the attacker. (4) Step forward with your right foot, stepping under the attacker as you raise his right arm up. (5) Go down slightly so you can bring your right arm over your head as you turn on the balls of your feet to face in the same direction as the attacker. Your fingers should always point in the direction you want your hands to go. (6) Lock the attacker's elbows and execute the throw by winding his arms in a circle as shown. There is no submission for this version since the attacker will have to release his hold as he's thrown.

2

3

5

6

Side Winding Throw (Yoko Makikomi)

This is a "safe" version of the preceding technique. (1) From the ready position, (2) your opponent grabs your wrists. (3) Bring your hands up inside the opponent's hands and toward him, locking his thumbs, and weakening his hold. (4) Turn both of your hands outward but don't grab his wrists yet. (5) Grab the op-

ponent's left wrist with your right thumb and index finger (C-grip) loose enough so your grip can slide around his wrist, and bring his right arm up. (6) Bring his left arm across his body, and C-grip his right wrist with your left hand. Your grip must be loose enough so that the opponent's wrist can slide.

Continued

7

8

(7) Bring his left arm up, crossing his arms, left over right, as you step under him with your right foot. Then, turn to your left on the balls of your feet. (8) At this point, tighten both C-grips, and wind his arms, (9) thus lock-

9

ing his elbows, and (10) throwing him. (11) Once the opponent is on the ground, (12) let go of his left wrist, turn, and drop your left knee onto his ear or cheek-bone for a finish.

Rear Circle Throw
(Ura Nage)

(1) From the ready position (tachi waza), (2) your attacker grabs both hands and pulls back. (3) Step back with your left foot, thus taking pressure off of his pulling. (4) Bring your right arm up over the attacker's head as you move your right foot back behind the attacker. (5) Moving your right foot back out of the way, bring the attacker's right arm down behind his head. (5A) Let the attacker keep hold of your hands. (6) Bring your hand and arm down in a circle behind the attacker to cause him to fall back. (7) If he hasn't let go of your left hand after he's been thrown, turn it out of his grip. (8) Drop your left knee down onto the side base of his ribs to finish him off.

Hand Throw
(Te Nage)
With Armlock Submission
(Ude Guruma)

(1) From the ready position, (2) the attacker grabs your wrists from behind. (3) Step back with your left foot, and turn to the attacker, lifting your left arm up slightly. (4) Maneuver your left hand behind you over to your right, (4A) grab onto the attacker's right hand with your left hand. (5) Turn your right hand out of the attacker's grip as you continue to face him. (6) Turn the attacker's

5

6

6A

right hand up so that you can start the hand throw (te nage). (6A) Try to have your thumb between his third and fourth metacarples (knuckles). (7) Bring your right hand up, and rest it on top of your thumb which is on the back of his hand. Do not grab his hand with your right hand. (8) Push the attacker's hand toward him with your right hand, further bending his wrist and hand

7

8

Continued

toward him, as you (9) pivot your left foot back to (10) execute the throw. (11) Be sure to turn your body in the same direction your left leg is pivoting (to your left). (12) Once the attacker is down, start to turn his wrist clockwise to your right to get him to turn over. (13) Slide your right hand down and grab his elbow. (14) Pivot your

right foot back as you pull his elbow to you, and continue to turn his wrist. (15) Step back with your left foot as the attacker turns onto his stomach. Set an armlock. (16) Go down onto your left knee so that your left thigh is against his locked forearm, helping to set the hold.

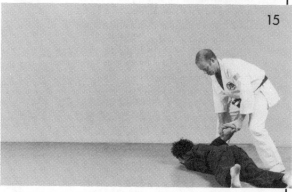

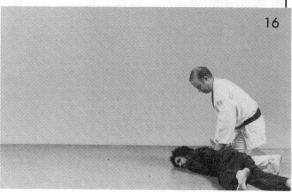

Rear Throw
(Ura Nage)

(1) From the ready position, (2) your opponent grabs your shoulder (gi) with his right hand and sets an armlock with his left hand. (3) Distract the attacker so that you can bring your arm down out of the armlock. (4) Bring your right foot around to your left as you turn to face the attacker, bringing youir arm up over the attacker's head. Let him keep hold of your wrist. Also, turn on the ball of your left foot so that your left foot is facing straight ahead. (5) Bring your hand down behind the attacker's head (6) to execute the rear throw (ura nage) and (7) bring the attacker down.

2

4

5

7

Forward Rear Throw
(Mae Ushiro Nage)
With Wristlock Submission
(Tekubi Shimi Waza)

(1) From the ready position, (2) your attacker thrusts with his knife. Block the attacker's forearm with a crossblock (juji), your right arm over your left. You should block with your lower forearms. Your hands should be open, but fingers and thumbs of each hand should be together. Step forward with your left foot about half a step at the same time to absorb the shock of the block. If you

don't step forward, your body will get knocked backwards by the force of the block, and you'll be off balance. (3) Maintain the block with your left forearm as you slide your right hand down, and (4) grab between the attacker's wrist and hand to keep his hand and knife from moving. (5) Step back with your right foot as you raise his right arm up. (6) Pivot back in with your right foot as you finish

 Continued

7

8

bringing his arm up, and (7) pull out, down, and back in a big circle to your right, (8) thus throwing the attacker. (9) Go down onto your left knee as the throw is completed. (10) Once the attacker is down, change your hold from (10A) the controlling grasp of his wrist to (11) a wrist lock, in preparation for the disarm. (11A) If he's still holding the knife, press

9

down on his wrist with his elbow on the ground. This will set and execute the (tekubi shimi waza) wristlock press submission. (12) Remove the knife from the attacker's hand. Always remove a weapon from your attacker before releasing him. Be sure to remove it from his immediate vicinity if you don't plan to use it (which isn't recommended).

Body Attack
(Atemi Shioku Waza)

(1) From the ready position, (2) pivot your right foot back to get your body out of the way of the knife thrust. (3) Grab his wrist from on top with your left hand, with your thumb resting between the third and fourth knuckle on the back of his hand. (4) Strike his hand to bend it with your right open hand, hopefully also causing him to lose the knife. (5) Bring your right foot forward and your right knee up (6) to strike the attacker in his solar plexus or the base of his sternum. (7) Bring your right foot down and execute a basic hand throw (te nage), (8) pivoting your left foot back and around in a counterclockwise circle (9) to finish the throw.

Reverse Winding Technique
(Gyaku Waza Makikomi)
With Shoulder Pin
(Senaka Shimi Waza)

(1) From the ready position, (2) pivot out of the way of the knife thrust by pivoting your right foot back. (3) Grab the back of the attacker's wrist and hand with your left hand as shown. Push his hand away from you as you step across him toward his left side with your left foot. (4) Turn to your right as shown. Also turn his hand to the right, palm up, as you turn your body. (5) For a standing armbar submission, step back with your left foot to block his left leg. Bring your right hand up under your left hand to add support to the hold. Lift his arm up, and bring it slightly toward your left as you tighten your body next to him, and turn to your right. (6) For a takedown, start with Step 4. Your right hand grabs hold of the back of his hand. Bring your left leg out and up, dropping your opponent onto his shoulder. (Go down slowly in practice.) Once the attacker is down, lift his straightened arm up toward his left shoulder for a shoulder pin submission, (senaka shimi waza).

Winding Armbar Takedown
(Ude Makikomi Shioku Waza)

(1) From the ready position, (2) your opponent attacks with a low knife swipe. Block the knife hand away by striking it with your left forearm as you step in slightly toward the attacker. (3) Push the attacker's forearm back with your left forearm as you bring your left hand up behind his upper arm. Pivot your right leg back clockwise as shown at the same time. (4) Continue to bring your hand to the back of his shoulder, forcing the attacker to bend over. (5) Bring your right hand up to the attacker's right shoulder, and (6) rest it on top of your left hand. Turn to your right on the balls of your feet and (7) drop down onto your left knee to bring the attacker down with an armlock as shown. (8) Remove the weapon from his hand.

2

4

5

7

8

133

Side Neck Standing Submission
(Kubi Shioku Waza)

(1) From the ready position, (2) your attacker attempts a stab to your middle. Step away from the upward swing by moving your left foot back as the attacker swipes and steps forward. (3) Bring your right arm up under his right arm with your body next to his right side. (4) Bring your right arm across to his left side, palm down, and reach around his back with your left hand. (5) Keeping his knife hand up by pinning his upper arm against your head and shoulder, make a fist with your right hand turned palm down. Clamp your left hand over your right hand, palm down. (6) Bring your right forearm sharply against the side of the attacker's neck below his ear with your radial styloid process (lower forearm), striking his neck. Pull toward you with your left hand. Make sure that your forearm is parallel to the side of his neck and perpendicular to his body. Maintain pressure until he drops the knife. Note: this technique could also be used for an overhead knife or club attack. The only difference is that you would step out to the side as in Step 2 and then block the downward swing of his right arm with your right shoulder as you step in for Step 3.

Outside Rear Sweeping Hip Throw
(Ura Harai)

This is a variation of the previous technique, where, after securing your hold on the attacker, you execute a rear throw. In this variation, (1) starting from the ready position, (2) your attacker attempts the upward sweeping strike with the knife. (3) Step away from the upward swing by moving your left foot back as the attacker swipes and steps forward. (4) Bring your right arm across to his left side, palm down, and reach around his back with your left hand. Keeping his knife hand up by pinning his upper arm against your head and shoulder, make a fist with your right hand turned palm down. Clamp your left hand over your right hand, palm down. Next, execute the rear throw, in this case, the outside rear sweeping hip throw (ura harai) by bringing your hips across the back of the attacker as for a basic hip throw (koshi nage). (6) Sweep his legs off the ground with an outside sweeping hip throw move (harai goshi) and (7) bring the opponent down onto the mat, (8) going down onto your right knee to retain control of the original hold. (9) To execute the hold as a submission, pull the attacker up into a sitting position and bring your right forearm sharply against the side of the attacker's neck below his ear with your radial styloid process (lower forearm), striking his neck. Pull towards you with your left hand. Make sure that your forearm is parallel to the side of his neck and perpendicular to his body. Maintain pressure while he drops the knife.

Sleeve Body-Drop Throw (Sode Otoshi) With Cross-Lapel Choke (Shimi Waza)

(1) From the ready position, (2) the attacker grabs your lapels for a cross choke (left over right) and sets the choke with his left forearm in your neck as he pulls your right lapel with his right hand. (3) Your right hand cups (sara) his left elbow (3A) with your fingers and thumbs pointing up in the direction your hand will go. Your left hand grabs his right sleeve. (4) As you roll his left arm up with your right hand, eliminating the choke, step in with your right foot, blocking his right foot, and pull his right sleeve. (5) Execute a

Continued

standard drop throw (tai otoshi), (6) dropping down onto your right knee to complete the throw. (7) Once the attacker is on the ground, his left lapel at mid-chest level with your right hand. Keep hold of his right sleeve with your left hand. You may now go into the cross-lapel choke submission (shimi waza). (8) Pull the attacker up into a semi-sitting position with your right hand. (9) Bring his right arm around in front of his face and (10) under his chin. (11) Pull his right arm across and against his chin or neck with your left hand as you pull his lapel across his throat with your right hand. He should be leaning against you. To make the submission more effective, you may extend your thumb into the cervical nerve, (just below his jawbone) or into the vagus nerve, (behind his jawbone and behind the front part of the second or third cervical transverse), or press the styloid process (just under his ear) at the same time.

7

8

10

11

Side Winding Throw
(Yoko Makikomi)

(1) From the ready position, (2) the attacker sets a cross choke (right over left). His right hand grabs high on your right lapel, and his left hand grabs just underneath on your left lapel. (3) Grab his right sleeve with your left hand. Keep your right arm down at your side at all times during the throw. (4) Turn counterclockwise into the attacker, holding his left arm tight so you can get tight against his body. By having your right arm at your side, you'll be better able to trap his right arm across his body. (5) Keep your body straight (don't bend over) as you step across him with your right foot and block his right leg as near to his ankle as possible. (6) Continue turning counterclockwise to your left to execute the side winding throw. Remember the basic rule: always look in the direction you're going, not at the attacker. Your body will follow. (7) To submit the attacker with an armlock, grab his right hand at the wrist with your right hand. (8) Your left hand then cups (sara) his elbow and rolls it forward (don't push against it—roll it) as you pull his arm back. (9) Go down onto your right knee as you finish the armlock with your opponent on his stomach.

Sleeve-Hold Knee-Drop Throw
(Sode Otoshi)

(1) Your attacker sets a low bearhug, pinning you at your elbows. (2) Reach over with your left hand and grab his right forearm. If he's holding you too tightly just drop slightly, and quickly to get some slack in the hold so you can grab his forearm or sleeve. Your right foot steps just to the outside of his right foot (3). Drop straight down onto your right knee as you turn to your left and pull his arm/sleeve with your left hand. You should step back with your right foot as you go down onto your right knee so that your kneecap is just in front of his right foot. This will keep him from stepping over your right leg as well as make the throw more effective. (4) Once the opponent is down, go into a wrist-twist submission (tekubi shimi waza), by (5) sliding your right hand to the back of his hand and hooking his forearm with your left hand as shown. (6) Twist his wrist away from you as you push down for the submission.

2

3

5

6

**One-Arm Drop Throw
(Ippon Otoshi)
With Neck Strangling Technique
(Kubi Shimi Waza)**

(1) Your attacker sets a bearhug from behind. (2) Stomp down onto his right instep with your right heel to distract him and loosen his hold. (3) As you put your right foot down, also crouch slightly. This will give you room to (4) raise your right arm up behind his right arm and (5) grab his right shoulder. (6) Drop

1

4

2

3

5

6

147

Continued

down onto your right knee, (7) pulling his shoulder with your right hand as you turn to your left (8) to execute the throw. (9) To execute the neck strangling technique (kubi shimi waza) submission, your left hand should be palm up. Be sure to keep hold of the attacker's gi at his shoulder with your right hand. (10) Slide your left hand under his left lapel as close to the left side of his neck as possible. (11) Grab his left lapel as high as possible, and get your hand and forearm under his chin. Pull with your right hand. This should set the choke by forcing your left hand and forearm against his neck as you pull his collar with your right hand. Do not push down with your left hand as it will defeat the strangling effect.

7

9

8

10

11

1

Outside Forward Finger Throw
(Mae Yubi Nage)
With Finger Press Submission
(Yubi Shimi Waza)

(1) Your opponent sets a full rear nelson. (2) To break the hold, (2A) grab one or two fingers with your right hand, (2B) and pull the finger(s) back. (3) Straighten his arm away to your right, and (4) turn to face the attacker. (5) Bring your left hand up, and grab three of his fingers. Be sure to keep his hand bent. (6) Move your right foot away from the attacker slightly, and turn on the balls of your feet so that you're facing the same direction as the attacker. (6A) Be sure his fingers are held correctly. You should be bracing (pushing) his fingers just below the knuckles with your hand at your index finger. (7) Push his hand slightly upward, out, and down in a big circle as you step forward with your right foot (8) to execute the throw. (9) To execute the finger press submission (yubi shimi waza), keep hold of his fingers as you throw him. Go down onto your left knee as the throw is completed. Put his palm down onto the ground, and quickly bend his fingers back to break them.

4

7

Hair-Grab Knee-Drop Throw
(Atama Otoshi)

(1) From a ready position, (2) your attacker brings his arms up in between yours to go into a full nelson. (3) Bring your hands up as you step your right foot back. (4) Grab the hair on the back of his head with both hands. Pull his hair and drop to your right knee, (5) bringing the opponent over your right shoulder (6) as you turn to your left. (7) Once your opponent is down, your right hand comes back. (8) Strike either his nose or right cheekbone with the base of your open hand for a quick finish.

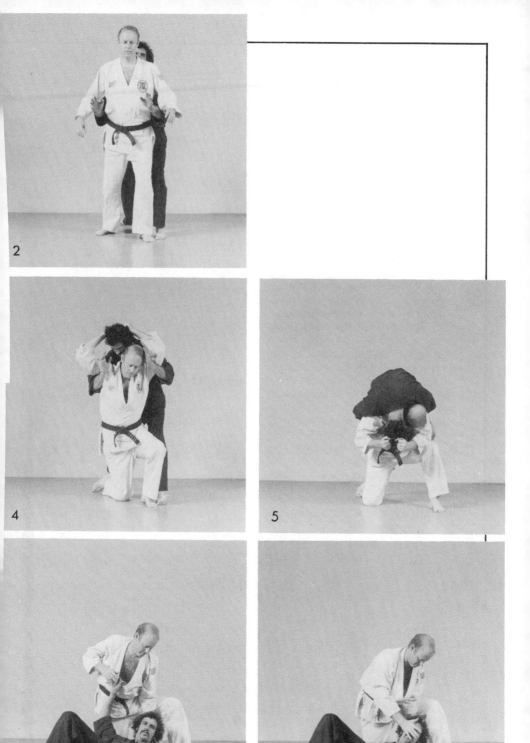

Left-Hand Throw
(Hidari Te Nage)

(1) From the ready position, (2) your attacker grabs your lapel with his left hand, and holds the knife against your stomach with his right hand. Never raise your arms any higher than chest level, if possible, in a weapons confrontation. Forearms and hands need to be this low to safely initiate techniques with minimum notice to the attacker. (3) Quickly turn to your right, blocking the knife hand away with your left forearm. Your right hand then comes up and (4) grabs the attacker's left hand with your thumb between his third and fourth knuckle (end of ulnar nerve). Turn it clockwise away from you. (5) Straighten out your left arm to keep the knife away from you. (6) Start the hand throw (hidari te nage) with your right hand, pushing his hand toward him as you pivot your right foot back in a clockwise circle and turn to your right. Bring your left arm up in a clockwise circle against the inside of the attacker's forearm to assist in the throw and to offer continued protection from the knife. (7) Move your left hand to assist the right hand in the execution of the hand throw once the throw is under way. (8) Once the opponent is on the ground, (9) raise your right leg and (10) strike any vital area on his head, or the side of his neck.

1

4

7

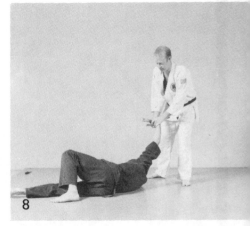

8

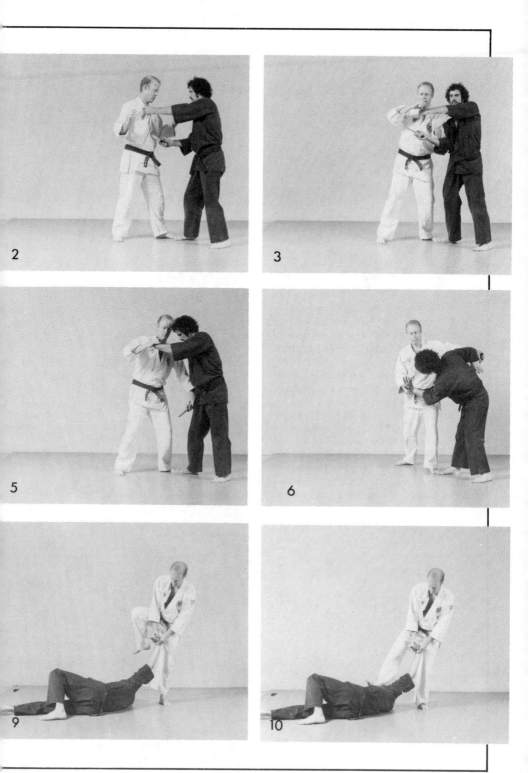

Face Attack
(Kao Tatake)

(1) An attacker has knife pointed at your throat, and you are backed up against a wall. (2) Quickly bring your right hand up under his knife hand with your palm facing you, and (3) cup (sara) his elbow with your left hand. (4) Quickly turn to your right, bringing the back of your right hand up against his knife hand, knocking it to your right. (5) As you turn your right hand to grab his knife hand at the wrist, (5A) roll his elbow upward. (6) Continue the elbow roll, slamming his face into the wall. (7) Grab his hair with your left hand and (8) pull back, throwing him to the ground.

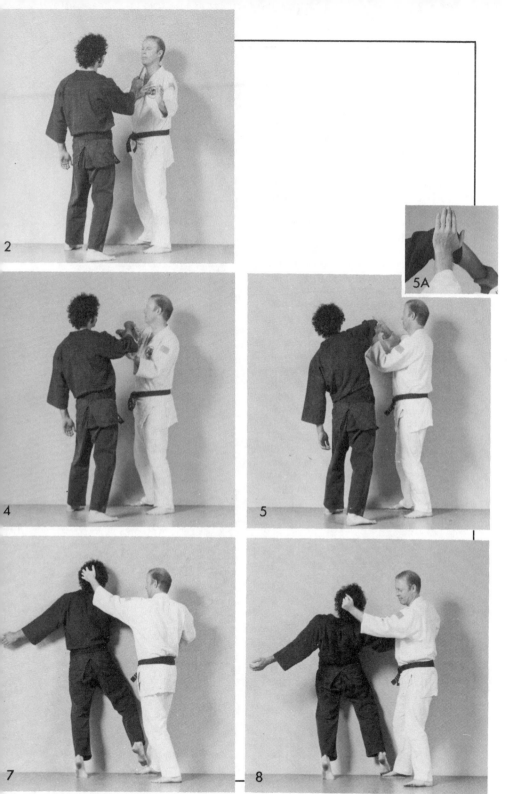

Hand Throw
(Te Nage)
With Wristlock-Lift Submission
(Tekubi Shimi Waza)

(1) From the ready position with the attacker's knife at your throat, (2) use your left forearm to strike his right forearm to your right as you quickly turn to your right. (3) Continue turning into the attacker. Slide your left hand down and grab his wrist and hand as for a regular basic hand throw (te nage). (4) Continue turning, using your body against the attacker's elbow, thus forcing him to hit the wall with the knife extended beyond your right upper arm. (5) Turn back around to your left to execute a standard basic hand throw (te nage). (6) Once the opponent is down, go into a wristlock lift submission (tekubi shimi waza). (7) Go down onto your right knee, and bring your right arm across the inside of his elbow. (8) Bend his hand down, thus bending his elbow. (9) Clamp your right fingers and thumb on top of your left forearm. (10) Pull up on the back of his hand with your left hand, keeping his wrist bent and his elbow pointing up for an effective submission.

1

4

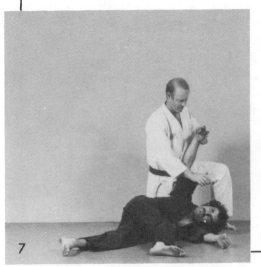

7

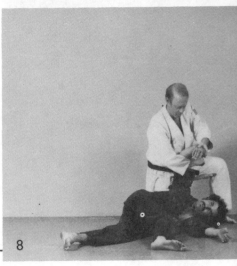

8

2

3

5

6

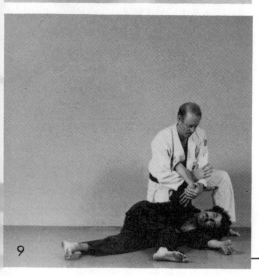

9

10

Nerve-Attack Armlock Takedown
(Shimi Waza)

(1) Your opponent has you in a head-lock set. (2) Bring your left hand up and (2A) C-grip the attacker's left wrist. (3) Bring your right hand up, palm up, and (3A) hook his fingers. (4) Your fingers pull toward you, turning his hand out of his grip as your left hand keeps his hand in the same position. (4A) Pull his arm down. (5) Step back with your right foot, getting out of the headlock, (5A) while keeping your hold of his wrist. (6) Bring the attacker's arm up into an armlock. (7) Let go of his fingers with your right hand, and grab his hair or collar, keeping pressure on the arm-lock, as your raise your right leg (8) strike the attacker behind his left knee-cap just hard enough to cause his leg to buckle. (9) Bring the attacker down onto his elbow, stepping back and go-ing down onto your right knee. Do this carefully in practice to avoid injury.

Thumb Attack
(Ube Shimi Waza)

(1) From your opponent's headlock set, (2) reach into his grasp with your right hand, and grab his right thumb placing your thumb at the base of his thumb. (3) Pull his thumb up and away (4) to release the headlock. (5) Keep hold of his thumb, bringing his arm up behind him. (6) Your left hand may assist in setting the armlock at this point. Make sure that his elbow is between your arm and your body for a proper lock. His thumb should be pointing downward with his palm toward his back. (7) Grab his thumb, and pull it back toward yourself as you also grab his hair, and pull back for the submission.

1

4

5

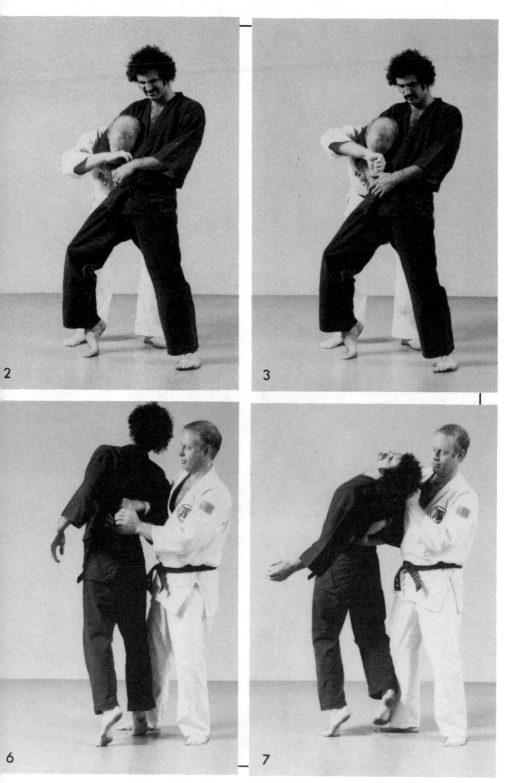

Wristlock Takedown
(Tekubi Shimi Waza)

(1) From the ready position, (2) your opponent grabs your left wrist with both of his hands. (3) Your left hand remains open, and turns clockwise around the outside of his right hand (4) to rest on the outside of his wrist, which should be turned up at this point. His wrist joint should be perpendicular to

the ground. (5) Grasp the back of his right hand with your right hand to keep him from taking it away. (6) Push down with your left hand, with your arm, and wrist straight, to execute the takedown. If done quickly, it will break your opponent's wrist, so take care in practice sessions.

Wristlock Takedown
(Tekubi Shimi Waza)

(1) From the ready position, (2) your opponent grabs your left wrist with his left hand. (3) Turn your left hand counterclockwise, coming up over the outside of his left wrist and forearm, turning his hand and wrist so his wrist is perpendicular to the ground, his thumb pointing

down. (4) Your right hand comes up and (5) rests on the back of his left hand to keep him from removing it. (6) Press down on his locked forearm with your left hand, keeping your left hand and arm straight to execute the takedown. Be sure to keep your posture straight.

Wristlock Come-along (Tekubi Shimi Waza)

(1) Your attacker grabs your hand as for a handshake. This is sometimes done to trap your right hand before an opponent hits you with his left. (2) Use your left hand to grab the attacker at his wrist with (2A) a loose C-grip, using your left thumb and index finger. (3) Step toward the opponent's right side with your right foot, keeping hold of his hand with both of yours. (4) Once

4

you have stepped in, pivot to your left on the balls of your feet and bring his arm over your head. This will twist (lock) his wrist. (5) Be sure to keep his hand and forearm vertical to the ground to maintain the lock. (6) To execute the forward come-along, lift his arm up slightly, and twist to create enough pain to get the opponent onto his toes.

5

6

Inside Forward Finger Throw (Mae Yubi Nage)

(1) From the ready position, (2) your opponent grabs your left wrist with his right hand. (3) Turn your left hand clockwise and up slightly in a small circle, (4) bending his wrist and continuing the

3

downward motion as you continue the circular motion. (5) Raise your right hand, with your thumb up and palm facing you, to the base of his fingers, and (5A) grab them as they lose their

4

5A

5

6

7A

7

grip on your wrist. (6) Turn your hand clockwise, away from you, so the attacker's hand is palm down and at his side. (7) Step forward with your right foot. Turn slightly to your left on the ball of your right foot, pivoting on the ball of your left foot. (7A) At the same time, raise his hand up by bending his fingers back. (8)

8

Once the attacker is on his toes from bending his fingers back, step forward with your left foot as you move your right hand up slightly, out in a big circle, and then down (9&10) to execute the throw. (11) Once the opponent is on the ground, execute a finger-press submission (yubi shimi waza).

CHAPTER 7
Reverses

There are ways to get out of almost any bad situation. The alternative may not always be the best, but sometimes it can give you some breathing space until you can remove yourself from the situation completely.

Reverse techniques operate the same way. They can give you some breathing space. These techniques are designed to counter a variety of judo throws and certain aikido holds in some cases. In the case of getting out of joint locks, you must be able to counter the lock or hold before it is set by your attacker. If it is set, and set as a *proper hold*, the only way out of it may be at the expense of seriously injuring the joint. It is essential that you execute these reverses slowly until you get a safe and complete feel for them. The alternative is to risk serious injury to yourself.

The basic premise behind reverse techniques is using your attacker's ki while he is using yours. For example, if your partner is about to throw you with a hip throw (*koshi nage*), and you're already on his back, you can very easily convert his throw to a reverse technique that will operate in your favor. As he is using your ki to throw you, all that is required of you is to hold onto his left shoulder with your left hand as he throws you. If you hold on to his left shoulder and turn so you'll land on your left side, your momentum will cause your partner to be thrown by yours and his ki combined. He should land at your left side, ready for submission.

In order for reverse throws to work well, they *must* be executed smoothly and with control. Trying to do them very slowly may be more of a safety hazard than working at a normal (but not fast) speed as your momentum for the technique is based on the momentum your opponent uses from you.

REVERSAL TECHNIQUES

Floating Drop Throw
(Uki Otoshi)

(1) From the ready position, grab your opponent by the collar. (2) As your opponent moves in to (3) execute a standard basic hip throw (koshi nage), (4) place your hand on his shoulder. (5) As you are lifted off the ground for the throw, grab your opponent's left shoulder, thus establishing control. (6) As your opponent completes the movement of the hip throw, (7) add your own momentum to the turn by maintaining your hold of your opponent's shoulder, thus throwing him and causing him to land at your left side on the mat. (8) Once he is thrown, move into a headlock pin, and (9) set it for a submission.

Shoulder Pull-Throw
(Senaka Hiki Nage)

(1) From the ready position, (2) you swing at your opponent, and your opponent blocks the attempted strike. (3) As your opponent moves in for a hip throw (koshi nage), (4) step around his right foot with your right foot. (5) Grab your opponent's right shoulder as you come around to his front, (6) falling toward his left side. Be sure to block your opponent's right leg with your left leg, and continue turning to your left as you fall, (7) thus throwing your opponent. (8) Once your opponent is thrown, go into (9) a headlock pin. Be sure your center of gravity is not resting on your opponent, your torso and legs are relaxed, and your feet are apart to spread your weight out as much as possible. You may also lower your head toward the right side of your opponent's head for a firmer pin.

Leg-Strike Rear Takedown
(Ashi Tatake)

(1) From the ready position, (2) grab at your opponent. (3) Your opponent deflects the attempted grab, and (4) moves in to (5) execute a drop throw (tai otoshi). (6) As your opponent sets up the throw, (7) grab the back of his collar, and place your right kneecap just behind your opponent's right knee joint. (8) Then, bend your opponent's knee joint with a slight push with your kneecap, thus breaking his balance and technique. Pull back his collar, and step back with your left foot to (9) execute a rear takedown. Be sure to get your left foot out of the way of your opponent's fall as you go down onto your right knee to complete the takedown. (10) Finish with a palm strike to your opponent's nose or cheekbone.

2

3

5

6

9

10

1

Sleeve-Pull Throw
(Sode Nage)

(1) From the ready position, grab your opponent by the collar. (2) Your opponent starts to (3) execute a standard hand throw (te nage). (4) As you are about to be thrown, (5) grab your opponent's right sleeve with your left hand, and (6) go down for the fall while holding on to your opponent's sleeve, and blocking his right foot with your left instep. (7) Your pulling his sleeve, plus the momentum of the throw, will cause your opponent to be thrown over your body. (8) As you block your opponent's right foot with your left instep, lift up on his right instep as he is going over you to enhance the reverse throw.

3

6

2

4

5

7

8

183

Shoulderlock Takedown
(Ude Guruma)

(1) From the ready position, grab your opponent. (2) Your opponent counters by removing your hand, and moving in (3) to set a standing figure-4 armbar ude guruma). (4) To break this hold, step in with your right foot, and (4A) bend your arm so that your palm is facing your opponent's back. (5) Slide your arm up, so that (5A) your elbow is above your opponent's forearm. (6) Then, bring your forearm down onto your opponent's shoulder joint, thus causing him to bend forward slightly. Your hand should be above your opponent's shoulder. (7) Your left hand then grabs on top of his right hand as he starts to go down. (8) Raise your right leg, and drop down onto his right rear side to execute the takedown, and (9) set the submission. Be sure to go down very slowly to avoid serious injury to your opponent.

CHAPTER 8

Applying Standing Techniques
to Ground Situations

L earning any system of self-defense from a standing position (on your two feet) is as basic as learning how to walk. Most attacks can be dealt with from a standing position. Many times, ground defenses can be avoided if a good standing defense is used. However, real life may not be so simple.

Many martial arts stress standing techniques only. They may give lip service to ground defenses and may even teach a few just to be able to prove they do. However, some martial arts do not give a proper emphasis to defending oneself while on the ground.

There are two major reasons why standing techniques are emphasized over ground techniques. Techniques are easier to teach, show, and learn from a standing positon. It is easy to move in the six primary directions (up, down, right, left, forward and backward) from a standing position. Also techniques executed from a standing position look cleaner than techniques executed while on the ground. They are more impressive, they can be executed with greater accuracy, and they have a better chance of attracting students. Both of these reasons for teaching standing techniques are valid.

Jujitsu is no exception to the two major reasons stated. Jujitsians like to look as good as any other martial art in this respect. We like to be able to accurately demonstrate techniques that will leave the attacker on the ground and the defender standing in a ready position, undaunted by the attack. No one wants to demonstrate defenses on the ground that don't have the same "flair" as standing techniques. Besides, it creates a negative impression to have to do techniques from the ground. There is the negative implication that the reason you're on the ground is because you did something *wrong* and have been forced to the ground. That's like starting out with two strikes against you. One: you did something wrong; and the second strike is because you did something wrong, so you're now on the ground.

Some martial arts ignore ground situations altogether or ignore them for all except advanced students. There is nothing wrong with this if the student realizes it and understands the consequences. All martial arts have their strengths and weaknesses. Not all martial arts styles cover every aspect of self-defense.

What *do* you do if you're on the ground though? You can't just lie there or think, "If I could only get onto my feet." You have to be able to defend yourself on the ground. It's the worst place to be and a difficult situation to get out of.

Fortunately, the art of jujitsu does have an extensive variety of ground defenses. It might be possible to write general books describing only jujitsu ground defenses. However, my purpose here is to provide you with the basic characteristics of effective ground defenses as well as provide some basic skills in the area.

All ground defenses have several characteristics in common regardless of the type of attack. Ground defenses must be simple to be effective. The more complex they are, the greater their chance of failure—not a good alternative if you're already on the ground. An effective ground defense must get your opponent off and away from you and prevent him from continuing his attack. Ground defenses rarely look *clean* or neat when compared to standing defenses. Because you can usually move only in three primary directions (left, right and up) and because you're already in close contact with the attacker, ground defenses tend to be generally unimpressive or they appear inefficient. Ground defenses *must* rely on the use of nerves, ki, and disturbing the attacker's balance (*kuzushi*). An attacker usually has weight and strength on his side. You can't resort to using those two items as you're often underneath him. Ground defenses must be done quickly for your own protection. You can't afford to mess around on the ground. Your defense must be quick, simple, effective, and capable of getting you out of the situation you're in.

One of the niceties of jujitsu is that many basic techniques that are done from a standing position can also be done prone on the ground. Many basic techniques that involve the use of the attacker's wrist, hand, and arm can be done on the ground with the attacker on you. Examples shown in the techniques that follow include *te nage* (hand throw), *te kubi shimi waza* (wristlock technique), and *ude guruma makikomi* (armbar winding throw). All of these can be executed from a prone position.

There are also a series of moves that can loosen up an opponent who is on you. These include a variety of nerve attacks, wrist and leg movements, and the use of the attacker's weight and leverage that will destroy his balance, thus making it possible to get out of harm's way and counter with an effective defense.

There are some ground attacks that have only one or two effective defenses. While there is nothing unique about the attack or the defense, the initial response by the defender must be specific. In the case of a face stomp, kick to the body, or body pin (face up or down), there are only a few things that can be done. You won't have much choice, but the defenses work.

In learning ground defenses you must have an open mind. Your mind must be flexible. You must develop a good working knowledge and understanding of basic jujitsu techniques, and try applying them to ground situations. Follow the five-step process in knowing a martial art as explained previously. The five steps (patience, repetition, understanding, experimentation, and evaluation) will make it possible for you to apply many techniques to ground situations.

Just keep one basic rule in mind. Ground defenses must be simple, quick, and effective to work. Don't develop techniques that have lots of moves, or will work only when specific conditions permit. Keep it simple and it will be more effective. The ground is the worst place to be. You don't want to be there any longer than you have to.

STANDING TECHNIQUES ADAPTED TO GROUND SITUATIONS

Wristlock Technique
(Tekubi Shimi Waza)

(1) The attacker attempts to choke you. The attacker could also be sitting on you. It makes no difference in the execution of the technique. In fact, the technique would actually work better if the attacker were sitting on you. (2) Bring your left hand over to your right as you turn to your right, and (3) hook onto the attacker's left hand with your thumb between his thumb and index finger, resting on the median nerve. (4) Push down with your thumb on the median nerve as you turn his hand away from you, bending his wrist. (5) Turn his hand in a counterclockwise circle to your left as you turn to your left. Try to keep his wrist bent as much as possible during the entire technique with pressure applied by your thumb, hopefully reaching the median nerve. (6) Bring your right hand up, and press in onto the back of the attacker's bent hand to bring him down with a wristlock takedown technique (tekubi shimi waza). (7) Once the attacker is down, (8) roll onto the attacker counterclockwise. Keeping his wrist bent, raise his arm up slightly for maximum effect of the wrist-press submission (tekubi shimi waza).

Head Winding Throw
(Atama Makikomi)

Execute this entire technique carefully to avoid serious neck injury. (1) The opponent chokes you. (2) Reach up with your left hand, and grab the hair on the back of his head. (3) Your right hand comes up cupped (sara), and rests on his chin. (4) Push with your right hand, and pull with your left, turning his head counterclockwise to your left, (5) as you turn to your left, (6) thus throwing attacker. (7) For submission, you may wish to snap his head back as he's going down or after he's down.

Armbar Winding Throw
(Ude Guruma Makikomi)

(1) An attacker comes in with a hit. (2) Reach up, and block his right arm away with your left arm. (3) Wrap your left arm around the attacker's right arm in a counterclockwise circle with your forearm under his elbow. Start to pull him down slightly as you go back down. (4) Your right hand clamps onto the attacker's right shoulder. Your left hand then clamps onto your right forearm. Make sure that your thumb and fingers are all on top of your forearm. If your thumb is underneath, you'll be grabbing your forearm, instead of using it as leverage. Then, you'll have to use muscle to execute the armbar. (5) Push down against his shoulder with your right hand and up against the backside of his elbow with your left forearm to set the armbar. At this point, you may apply the submission and/or dislocate the attacker's elbow, or (6) execute the throw. (7) You may submit the attacker with the figure-4 armbar, dislocating his elbow if done quickly from this position.

2

5

Elbow Roll
(Hiji Waza)

(1) You're on the ground, and the attacker comes in with a strike. (2) Turn to your left, and deflect the strike outward to your right with your right forearm. (3) Turn back down onto your back as you slide your right forearm down his forearm, and use your right hand to grab (4) his wrist with your thumb underneath. (5) Cup (sara) your left hand under his elbow. (6) Note that your left fingers should be extended, thus extending your ki. Roll his elbow, thus bending it as you turn to your right. (7) Continue turning his elbow, (8) thus bringing the attacker (9) down onto his right shoulder.

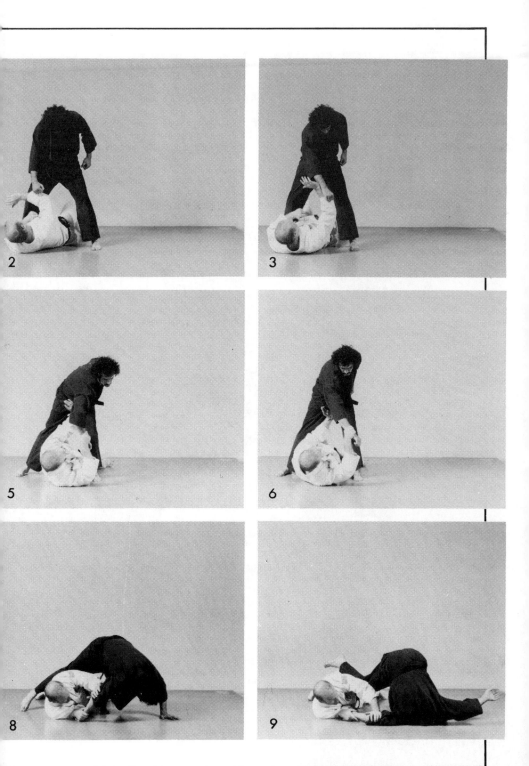

CHAPTER 9
Ground Defenses

As stated earlier in this book, the worst place to be is on the ground with an attacker over you. It's also a situation that you'll want to get out of as fast as possible. Ground techniques do not have the same flair as standing techniques, but they do work well when executed properly. This is an area you should work on to round out your education in jujitsu.

The 11 ground defenses shown in this section can be divided into two subcategories. The first seven techniques are designed specifically for certain attacks while you're on the ground. They are extremely effective and should be executed slowly as there is a great deal of joint locking and twisting involved. The last four techniques are actually modifications of techniques that can be used while in a standing position. They don't have the same flair as do similar standing techniques but they are excellent examples of how basic techniques can work whether you're on your feet or the ground. With practice, you will probably find other standing techniques that work well on the ground—although, perhaps not as neatly.

DEFENSIVE GROUND TECHNIQUES

Foot-Grab Body-Roll Elbow Strike
(Ashi Tatake)

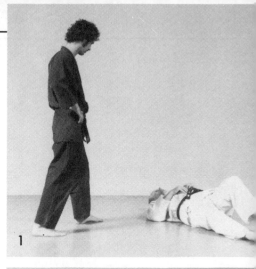

(1) Your opponent is standing next to you. (2) He comes in with a kick to your side. (3) Bring both of your forearms down against your chest with your hands into fists, and bring your knees up to protect your body. (4) Turn toward the attacker as he makes contact. (5) Open your right hand, and hook behind his right ankle from the inner side of his foot, trapping it. If he kicked with his left foot, you would hook around his left ankle from the outer side of his foot with your right hand. (6) Quickly roll into the attacker, putting your entire body weight against his knee as you hold his foot with your right hand. If you do this quickly, it is possible to lock his knee-cap and break his leg—so be careful. This motion will cause the attacker to fall backwards. (7) Once the attacker is down, keep turning. Your right hand lets go of his ankle, and goes back into a fist with your palm facing you. (8) Continue to roll your body, striking down with your right elbow (9) into the attacker's groin or lower abdomen.

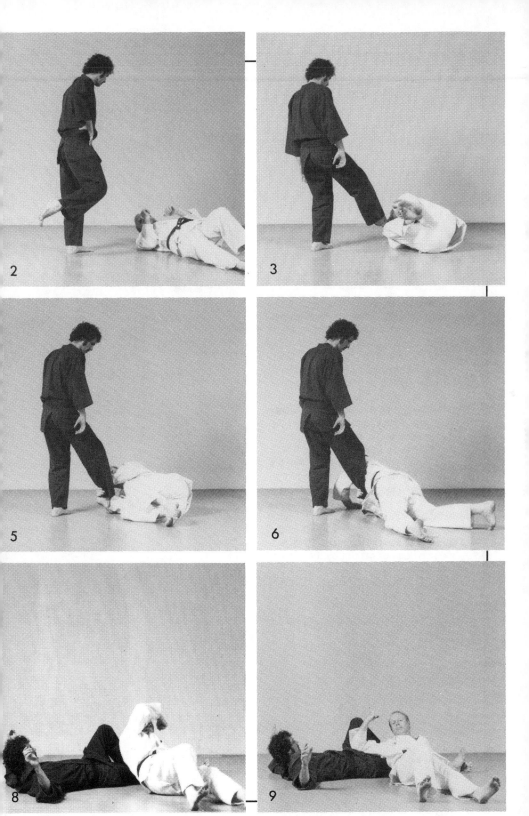

Foot-Twist Throw
(Ashi Makikomi)

(1) From the ready position, you are on the ground, and the attacker is over you. (2) The attacker comes in for a foot stomp to your head. Bring both forearms up over your face, and clench your fists for added strength and support. (3) As the attacker's foot comes down, block the foot with your forearms. (4) Then, grab the attacker's heel with your right hand, and (5) then the ball of the same foot with your left hand. (6) Push the attacker's heel with your right hand, and pull the ball of his foot with your left hand in a counterclockwise direction, as you roll to your right to (7) execute the throw. (8) Once the attacker is down, your left foot comes over and (9) strikes down on the attacker's anus, thus causing a momentary loss of control by the sphincter muscles.

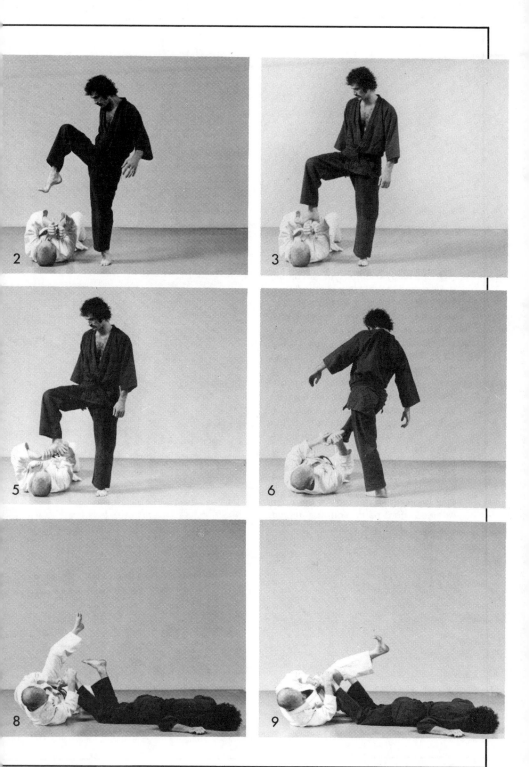

Ankle-Grab Kneelock
Rear Throw and Groin Strike
(Ura Nage)

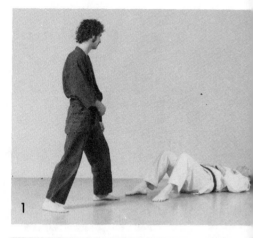

(1) In the ready position, you are on the ground, and the attacker is standing at your feet. (2) The attacker grabs both of your feet, and pulls them, dragging you. (3) Bend your legs, thus bringing yourself close to the attacker's feet. Do not *try* to sit up at any time. (4) Grab behind the attacker's ankles with your hands from the outside of his feet. Bring your legs up to the outside of his hips, (5) locking his legs, and (6) causing him to fall backwards. The momentum of his falling backwards will bring you up into a sitting position if you keep hold of his ankles. Once you are sitting up, (7) strike the attacker in his groin with your left fist. (8) As he sits up in reaction to your groin strike, hit him in the nose with your right palm. You may repeat the last steps if you wish.

2

4

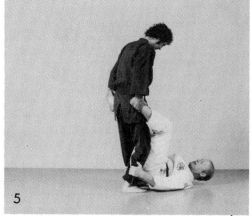

5

7

8

Reverse Stomach Throw
(Gyaku Tomoe Nage)

(1) From the ready position, you are on the ground, and the attacker moves in. (2) The attacker grabs your wrists, and drags you on the ground. (3) Turn your right hand clockwise and left hand counterclockwise, so you can grab the attacker's wrists from the outside. Pull down on his arms, bending your arms, and bringing yourself closer to the attacker as he continues to pull. This will also cause him to bend forward slightly. (4) Bring both of your feet up into the attacker's stomach, and pull his arms down to set the throw. (5) Straighten your legs out, bringing them down, thus throwing the attacker over you and (6) onto his back. (7) Once the attacker is down, (8) raise your left foot, and (9) strike down on his sternum with your left heel.

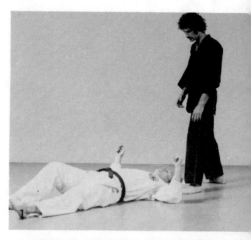

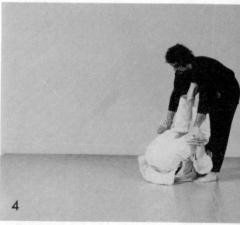

4

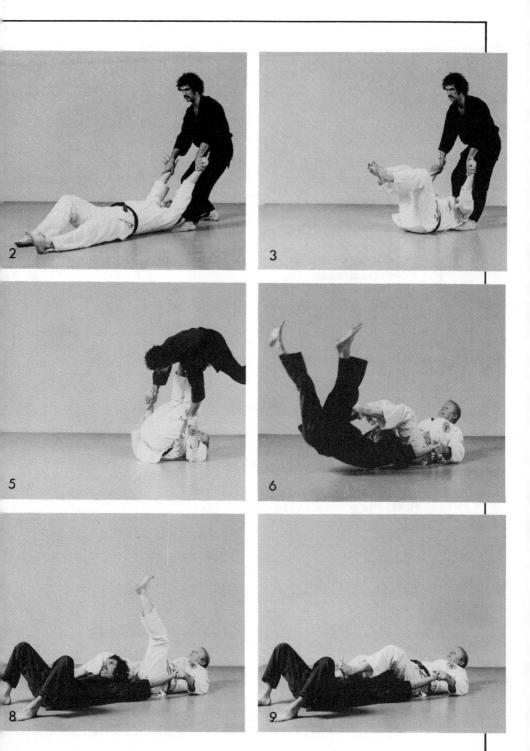

Kneelock Rear Throw
with Crotch Strike
(Ura Nage)

(1) The attacker is over you, ready to attack. (2) Your left and right hands hook onto the back of his ankles from the outside of his feet. (3) Bring your left leg up between his legs and (4) around to the side of the attacker's right leg. (5) Bring your leg up toward his hip, locking his kneecap, and (6) push back against his upper leg, thus causing him to fall backward. (7) As the attacker falls, be sure to bring your right leg up through his legs for the finishing strike as well as to prevent his body from landing in your foot. (8) Once the attacker is down, bring your right leg all the way up, and then strike his crotch with your heel. Be sure to keep hold of his feet.

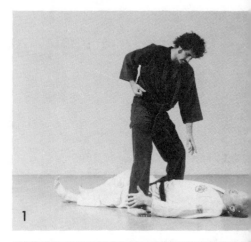

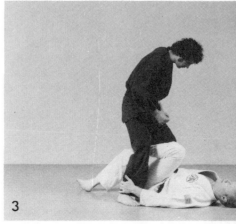

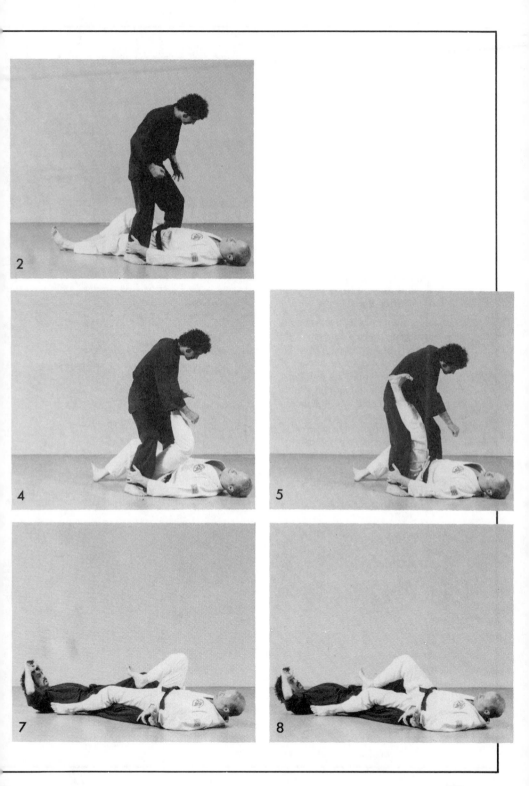

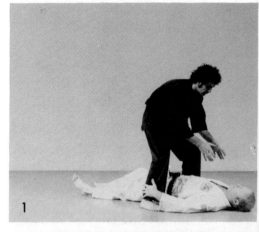

Kneelock Rear Throw
with Groin Strike
(Ura Nage)

(1) The opponent comes in with an attack as you grab both of his ankles. (2) Bring both of your legs up (3) through his legs, and (4) rest them on his upper legs. (5) Straighten your legs out, locking his knee joints, and push back with your legs, causing him to fall backward. Keep hold of his feet and (6) the momentum of his fall will bring you up into a sitting position. (7) Strike the attacker's groin with your left hand. (8) As he sits up, strike to his nose or cheekbone with the heel of your palm.

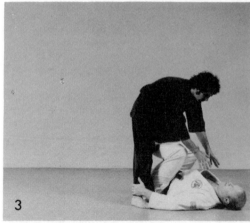

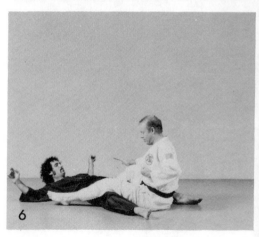

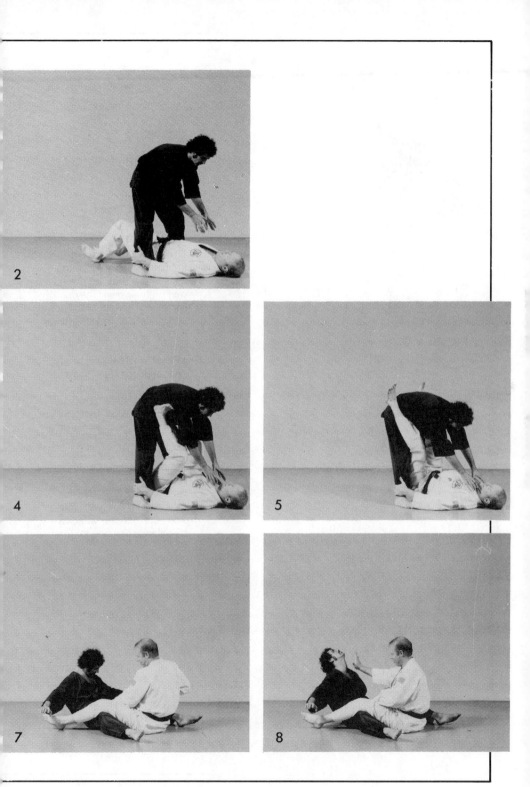

Butt Thrust with Thumblock Lift (Ube Shimi Waza)

The butt thrust and thumblock lift are separate techniques that will work well on their own. They are combined here for added effect. Do *not* execute the butt thrust portion of this technique if you have any sort of back problem. (1) Your opponent is sitting on you, pinning your arm. (2) Slide your hands down to your sides. Don't try to lift them. Keep your palms up as you slide your hands. This will shift your opponent's balance. (3) Bring your heels as close to your butt as possible. Moving your hands down to your side has put the attacker off balance. Be sure to turn

4

your head to the left or right by this time. (4) Bring your hands and arms up the sides of the attacker, palms up, locking his thumbs, and bringing him over you. (5) Thrust up with your butt at the same time. (6) Your opponent should roll to avoid a possible broken collarbone. This techniques is very effective for a rape situation in which your head is near a wall or other hard surface. Although you may not force your attacker completely over you, the technique will cause his head to strike the wall or hard surface. Then roll away.

5

6

CHAPTER 10

Reversing Holds and Pins on the Ground

Not all assailants will take the opportunity to hit or kick you while you're on the ground. Some, particularly if they have a judo or wrestling background, prefer to hold or pin their opponent down. Some people feel safer executing a good pin- or hold-down—and they probably are. However, since you don't care for either situation, I'm sure you'd much rather be in control of your attacker than the other way around.

The three reversals in this chapter are designed to be used against some of the more common pins and hold-downs used in judo. Judo people are exceptionally strong in this area, and spend a considerable amount of time in perfecting their mat techniques. The three reverses are selected out of the many more I have learned, to help you develop a better understanding of the use of leverage in getting out from under your opponent.

TECHNIQUES FOR REVERSING HOLDS AND PINS ON THE GROUND

Reversing a Headlock Pin

(1) Your opponent sets a headlock, and (2) puts his head down next to yours to maximize his ground weight distribution. (3) Turn into your opponent so that your body is next to his. Raise your left leg and arm. (4) Hook your left leg over his left leg. (5) Start to pull your opponent over you with your leg. Bring your left hand up between your head and his, and rest it on his chin. (6) Turn, don't push, his chin away from you as you continue to turn to your left and pull him over with your left leg. (7) Roll the attacker over you, (8) thus getting out of the headlock, and putting the opponent on the mat face down. (9) Set a reverse headlock by slipping your left hand under his neck, and clamping onto your left forearm or wrist with your right hand. (10) Don't lift up the headlock. Lean back on his head with your body as the headlock is set. Make sure the line of your body is perpendicular to his body for greater security.

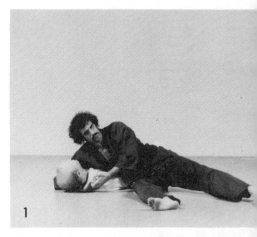

1

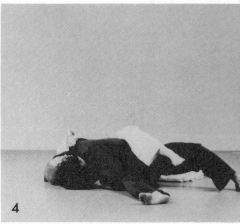

4

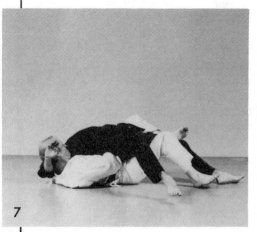

7

8

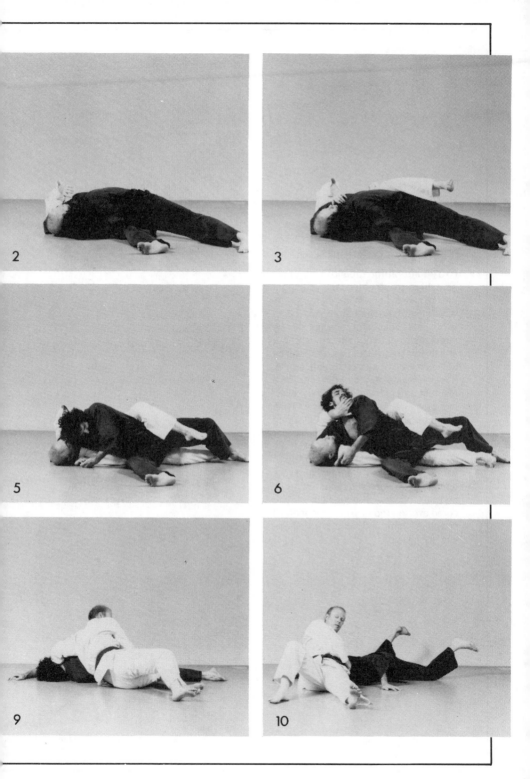

Reversing an Attempted Figure-4 Armbar Submission

(1) You are on the ground. Your opponent tries to strighten out your right arm to set a figure-4 armbar. This reverse must be done before your opponent gets your arm straight. If he manages to get your arm straight, but still hasn't set the lock, you may still be able to reverse it by moving your arm in, pushing your elbow joint beyond where his right arm crosses yours, thus relieving pressure from your elbow. Then continue with this technique. (2) Bring your right forearm up, and (3) move your right hand to (4) rest on the back of his head. (5) Rest your left hand on top of your right hand as you turn toward your opponent. (6) Push with your left hand, and pull down with your right as you come over on top of your opponent, (7) straddling him, and setting a half-nelson submission.

2

4

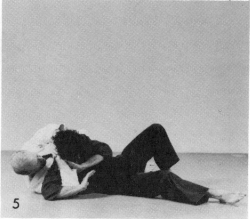

5

7

Reversing a Cross Body-Drop Pin

(1) You are on the ground. (2) Your opponent jumps onto you. Your hands should be palm up. Be sure to *kiai* (shout) loudly as he lands on you. This will get the air out of your lungs and allow your ribs to flex. If he lands on you with your lungs full, you won't be able to do anything except try to get your breath back. (3) As the opponet lands on you, grab the skin and subcutaneous fat layer on the side of his body with both of your hands and dig in with your finger tips. This is a very sensitive part of the body, and if you do this quickly, your opponent will go up and away from your body to

get away from the pain of your double grip, making the rest of the technique easier to accomplish. Bring your legs up to as close to your rear as possible. (4) Maintain your hand grips on the attacker's side. Thrust your butt up, arching your back as you thrust. (5) Roll the attacker over your head, lifting up your arms to help the throw and (6) clear his body from your head. As you raise your arms, maintaining the grip, your opponent, to get away from your painful grip, may not make any contact with your head at all. But, make sure to turn your head to the side for safety anyway.

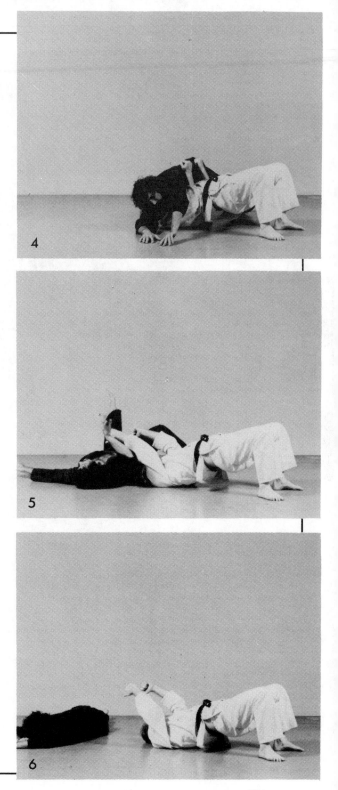

CHAPTER 11
Staff/Baton Defenses

Proficiency in the use of baton and staff defenses is an optional area to be tested at the *nikyu* or higher level. The purpose for including such defenses is to help the student become aware that he can successfully defend himself against quite a number of weapons that might be used against him. The baton, hanbo (30 inch), and jo (48 inch) are excellent weapons with which to start exploring this concept. The techniques presented will also further develop the student's ability to use his attacker's ki even though it may be extended into a weapon.

As a word of caution, you should also be aware that a person skilled in the use of a baton, hanbo, or jo may also know effective (and painful) counters to the techniques shown here. Many of the techniques of the hanbo, jo, and baton are based on empty-hand techniques shown in this book and *Jujitsu: Basic Techniques of the Gentle Art*. This is another area into which you may wish to branch out as you continue your studies in the art of jujitsu.

TECHNIQUES FOR DEFENDING AGAINST STAFF OR BATON

Forward Throw
(Bokken No Tatake Mae Nage)

(1) From the ready positon, (2) the attacker lunges at you with a straight thrust. Start to move your hands, left palm up and right palm down. As you (3) pivot your right leg back in a circular motion to your right to get out of the direction of the baton's thrust. (4) Bring your right hand down on the front end section of the staff, and bring your left hand up at the other end. (5) Your right hand grabs the front section of the staff. Your left hand remains open. Move the staff in a clockwise circle, thus starting the throw. (6) Grab the rear section of the staff once it passes you, assuring your control of the staff as (7) the throw is completed. (8) Remove any hold the opponent may have of the staff by quickly pulling up once the opponent is on the ground. (9) Untwist your crossed arms, raise the staff up, and (10) strike down with the end of the staff to a nerve center—solar plexus, or sternum.

Inside Forward Throw
(Naka Mae Nage)

(1) Get set in the ready position. (2) As the attacker thrusts, pivot your right leg out and away to your right. Your left hand is palm down, and your right hand should be palm up. (3) Once the staff passes your body, clamp your hands onto the end sections of the staff, just outside of his hands. (4) As you start to bring the front end of the staff down, pull the rear end of the staff across the attacker's body and out behind his left arm with your right hand. (5) Establish a firm grip on the staff with your left hand. Once the opponent lets go of the rear section of the staff, or even if he doesn't, open up your left hand, and have it rest lengthwise with your fingers pointing toward the rear of the staff. Step forward with your right foot. (6) Push the rear of the staff forward in a circular motion against his upper arm with your right hand. Pull the staff to your left side and up in a ciruclar motion to execute the throw. (7) The opponent will land on his shoulder, or on his back, if thrown completely over. (8) Bring the baton up, and (9) strike down to the kidneys.

Stomach Throw (Bokken Tomoe Nage)

(1) From the ready position, (2) your opponent pushes with the staff. Your hands come up. (3) Grab with both hands on top of the attacker's hands, (3A) thus trapping his hands on the staff. (4) As the attacker continues to push against you,

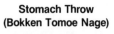

4

bring your right foot up to his lower stomach at the balance point (saiki tanden) as you start to fall back. (5) Continue this movement. Once you are on the ground and your foot is against his stomach, (6) push with your

5

6

Continued

7

8

right foot, (7) lifting the opponent off the ground, and (8) executing a stomach throw (tomoe nage). (9) Once the opponent is on the ground, (10) turn to your

9

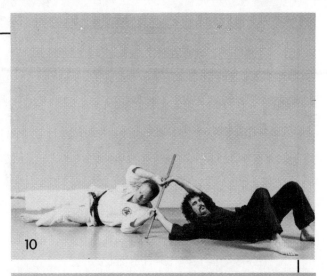

10

left, and (11) come up onto your left knee and right foot. (12) Remove the staff from the attacker's grip, and strike down with the end into a vital area.

11

12

1

Side Throw
(Bokken No Tatake Yoko Nage)

(1) From the ready position, (2) the attacker moves in to push against you with the staff. (3) Bring your right forearm up, and block the staff just inside his left hand. Your left hand then grabs the end section of the staff just outside of his right hand. Do not grab the staff with your right hand until the opponent is down. (4) As the opponent continues to push, turn the staff in a counterclockwise circle, pulling with your left hand, and pushing with your right forearm (5) as you pivot your left foot back. (6) Continue the counterclockwise circle of the staff, bringing your left hand toward your left side to (7) finish the execution of the throw. Be sure to turn your body to the left as you execute the throw. (8) Once the opponent is down, remove the staff from his grip if he's still holding it, and (9) strike down to a vital area.

4

7

Thumblock Takedown
(Ube Shimi Waza)

(1) Get set in the ready position. (2) As your opponent pushes with the staff, bring your hands up to rest against his hands. (2A) His fists are resting in your palms with your thumbs extended inward. (3) Raise the staff up slightly, if possible, as you (3A) grab over his thumbs with your thumbs. (4) Clamp your fingers down over his fists, as you start to turn the staff toward him, thus bending his wrists back. (4A) Note how your thumbs are holding his thumbs against the staff. This is what establishes control over the opponent and creates the pain, thus making the takedown possible. (5) Roll the staff back and (5A) down toward the opponent, (6) thus bringing the attacker down as far as you wish. You may strike him in the chest or face with your kneecap as you bring him down. Remove the staff from his grasp once he's down.

2

3

5

6

CHAPTER 12

Technique/Attack Cross-Reference Chart

You should realize by now that a single jujitsu technique can be used for a variety of different attacks. Very few techniques apply only to specific attacks. More commonly, the basic technique will be modified in some small way to adapt to the attack.

For example, in this book a shouder-grab rear throw is shown for a single hit attack. Look at the following chart and find this technique. If you move across the chart you will notice an (x) which indicates that the technique is shown for a single hit. You will also notice that there are checks (✓) under single lapel grab, rear shoulder grab, double hit, overhead and sideswipe clubs, overhead knife, and grab and hit indicating the technique can also be used for these attacks. To alter the shoulder-grab rear throw for a lapel grab, you would have to get the attacker's hand off your lapel by using a nerve attack, leverage, hit, or other distraction before going into the throw. For a double hit, you'd only have to execute as for a single hit, deflecting his right attacking hand to your right. In doing so, the movement of his right arm across his body will negate his left-handed second punch.

This modification process could be applied to any of the techniques shown in this book. Because of this, and assuming that you're going to work on these modifications, the actual number of techniques that you could learn from this book far exceeds those shown. Although there are 35 techniques presented on this chart there are 152 modifications of these techniques also possible. Although there are some occasions where a basic or intermediate technique may be repeated in the test of *Jujitsu: Basic Techniques of the Gentle Art* or *Jujitsu: Intermediate Techniques of the Gentle Art,* neither book could show all of the variations. You should work to develop other modifications on your own.

Thus, the purpose of this chart is to help by showing you what additional attacks the techniques can be used for. By the time you start using this chart, your "loosening up" techniques, (blocks, nerve attacks, hits, kicks, and other distractions,) should be fairly well-established so that you can modify the techniques to fit the attack.

This chart shows specific techniques in this book that can be applied to a variety of attacks. While there would be no modification in the actual execution of the specific technique, it would be necessary to modify your initial response (for example, block, release, strike, etc.) to the specific attack from what was shown in the text.

x = Technique shown for this attack.

↙ = Technique can also be used for this attack.

DIFFERENT

INTERMEDIATE JUJITSU TECHNIQUES	single lapel grab	double lapel grab	front choke	rear choke	rear forearm choke	headlock	rear shoulder grab	rear bearhug	fron...
Shoulder Grab Rear Throw	↙						↙		
Elbow Rear Throw	↙	↙	↙						↙
Double-Strike Turning Throw	↙	x	↙						
Multiple Strike Belt Throw	↙	↙					↙		
Floating Drop Throw	↙	↙	↙				↙		
Foot-Twist Side Throw									
Leg-Winding Throw									
Wrist Side Throw									
Wrist Side Throw–Striking Technique									
Side Winding Throw (No. 1)									
Side Winding Throw (No. 2)									
Rear Circle Throw									
Hand Throw	↙	↙	↙	↙		↙			
Rear Throw									
Forward Rear Throw									
Body Attack	↙	↙	↙						
Reverse Winding Technique	↙	↙	↙						
Winding Armbar Takedown									
Side Neck Standing Submission									
Outside Rear Sweeping Hip Throw									
Sleeve Body-Drop Throw		↙							
Side Winding Throw		↙							
Sleeve-Hold Knee-Drop Throw				↙	↙		↙	x	
One-Arm Drop Throw				↙	↙		↙	x	
Outside Forward Finger Throw				↙	↙	↙			
Hair-Grab Knee-Drop Throw				↙				↙	
Left-Hand Hand Throw	↙	↙	↙	↙		↙			
Face Attack									
Hand Throw	↙	↙	↙						
Nerve-Attack Armbar Takedown						x			
Thumb Attack						x			
Wristlock Takedown (No. 1)									
Wristlock Takedown (No. 2)									
Wristlock Come-Along									
Inside Forward Finger Throw									

TYPES OF ATTACKS

single hit	double hit	overhead club	sideswipe club	overhead knife	straight knife	knife swipe	knife threat	handshake	wrist grab	kick	push	grab & hit	mugging	arm grab	ground attack	cross choke	rear nelson	hair grab
X	✓	✓	✓	✓								✓						
✓	✓	✓	✓	✓	X	✓		✓	✓		✓							
✓	✓	✓						✓	✓			✓						✓
X	✓	✓	✓						✓		✓	✓						
X	✓	✓	✓					✓	✓		✓	✓						✓
										X					✓			
										X								
									X									
									X									
	✓								X						✓			
	✓								X						✓			
									X									
✓	✓	✓	✓	✓	✓	✓	✓	✓	X			✓			✓			
									X									
	✓			X				✓	✓									
	✓	✓	✓	X	✓							✓						
	✓	✓	✓	X				✓	✓		✓	✓						
					X			✓	✓									
✓	✓	✓	✓	✓														
✓	✓	✓	✓	✓														
	✓															X		
	✓															X		
													✓					
													✓					
													✓				X	
													✓				X	
✓	✓	✓	✓	✓	✓	✓	X	✓	✓			✓			✓			
✓		✓		✓			X					✓						
							X					✓						
									X									
									X									
✓							X		✓									
✓	✓	✓							X									

CHAPTER 13
Testing for Higher Ranks

Jujitsu: Basic Techniques of
the Gentle Art sought to
bring the beginning jujitsu
student to approximately the *yonkyu* (fourth) level of knowledge in jujitsu. It provided some basic theory plus quite a bit of technical knowledge.
If the student began to develop a working knowledge of the theories plus
the ability to combine and vary techniques to the wide spectrum of attacks
listed in the glossary, he would be well on his way toward intermediate
growth in the art.

As stated earlier, the purpose of this book is to bring the *mudansha*
(novice) up to shodan level in the same two areas: technical knowledge and
theory. We will review some of the general concepts and some of the
more important subjective elements that are considered in a promotion

to *sankyu* (third) or higher grades.

At the brown belt (*sankyu, nikyu, ikkyu*) level we can look at the general and specific requirements. As we look at the general criteria, we are immediately faced with a philosphical question. The issue is this: a brown belt should have a working knowledge of all the kata listed and be able to demonstrate effective defenses for all the attacks listed. It is possible to require the candidate to demonstrate all of the kata and waza. Some systems of jujitsu require that a candidate for a particular belt demonstrate all of the knowledge he has acquired up to that point. That is to say that a person testing for sankyu would have to go through the rokyu and yonkyu exams in the process of testing for sankyu. The advantage of testing is that it does ascertain whether the candidate has a complete knowledge up to the level he's testing for. The other side of the coin is that this format is very time consuming and physically exhausting for a person testing for sankyu and higher grades. (It should be noted that there is not anything necessarily wrong with a test being physically exhausting. The yonkyu test, if done properly, usually is.)

There is a second type of testing that can be done that is perhaps just as effective. It's called random testing. In this format, the candidate is expected to show ten kata and 15 waza from the brown belt tests. The only problem for the candidate is that he doesn't know which kata or waza he'll be expected to execute until he's told to execute them during the test. While this format is not physically exhausting or as time consuming, it does cover the same material. It also allows the examiner to be more critical in his observation of the candidate. A person who has been doing kata and waza for half-an-hour or more isn't going to be doing them as well as a person who is requred to demonstrate randomly selected items over a 10-20 minute period. Most tests in any subject area only test on a random basis. There is no reason why this format shouldn't apply to the martial arts.

Random testing of kata and waza is done at the sankyu and higher levels for three reasons. The examiner is interested to see what the student can do on a random basis. Techniques selected at random require that the student know the kata or waza independently of other kata or waza. There is no security in knowing that after one kata comes another specific kata; there is no order to the testing. Also the student is expected to provide a better quality demonstration of his knowledge as he has the security of knowing that he'll only have to perform "x" kata or waza. Finally, as he doesn't know specifically what he will be tested on, he must know everything that he might be tested on. This assures quality and the recognition by the student that his knowledge must be complete.

Testing for Brown Belt

Thus, the first general requirement at the brown belt level is that the student must have an understanding of *all* the kata and waza required at the brown belt level.

The candidate should be developing an effective and personalized self-defense system. Even though technical knowledge of a large number of kata and waza is required, this does not mean that all of the kata would be used in a personalized self-defense system. Any student in any martial art has certain pet techniques; techniques he can do extemely well and work best for him. The same is true in jujitsu. Some techniques work better for some people than others. Students, regardless of rank, will usually resort to these techniques in spontaneous situations. This also leads to the third of the general criteria.

In addition to the first two requirements the brown belt candidate should be able to react automatically to attacks without any hesitiation. In a street situation a rapid response is essential to survival. Developing automatic reactions is a skill that, once learned, can also be controlled. Only if defenses can be executed automatically, without conscious thinking, will they be of any real value on the street.

The candidate should be able to demonstrate a wide knowledge of techniques to specific attacks. Flexibility is a watchword in jujitsu. A student who can modify and combine techniques to suit his needs is mastering the art of flexibility. Once basic techniques are learned, the serious student is limited only by his imagination. Techniques should be kept simple. The more complex the technique, the less its chance for success.

The last general requirement has to do with the student's attitude. The student's attitude should be evaluated in the following five areas: 1) self-respect and respect for others, 2) humility and confidence, 3) desire for self-improvement, 4) a willingness to help others, 5) loyalty to the dojo and the instructor.

It is impossible to respect others if you don't respect yourself. Thus a successful jujitsu student should be developing his self-respect. He will see himself as a person of worth, with capabilities and skills that are worthwhile. If a student respects himself he will also develop a sense of confidence. He will know that he can learn new skills, be successful, be worthy of the respect of others, and be willing to explore new areas of his life. Self-confidence should not be confused with conceit. If a person has self-respect and self-confidence, he will also be humble. This humility shouldn't be seen as subservience, though. Humility means recognizing your skills and abilities, but not flaunting them for others to see, or abusing the skills and knowledge you have acquired. It means treating other people with at least the same courtesy and respect you would like them to extend to you.

In addition to these three *subjective* areas, a serious student should also be demonstrating a continuous desire for self-improvement, a willingness to help others inside and outside the dojo, and loyalty to the dojo and instructor. The last three areas are important as they are a reflection of the first three. If a student is respectable, respectful, confident, and humble then he will also be able to succeed in these three areas. Success in one will lead to success in the others.

In this chapter, you will find the specific requirements for promotion to each kyu level, including sankyu, nikyu, and ikkyu. You should become familiar with all of the requirements so you will be able to strive toward your goal more efficiently.

Testing for Shodan

Securing the rank of *shodan* (first degree black belt) is an important step in the growth of a jujitsu student. It is at this stage that the student changes from a *mudansha* (below black belt) to *yudansha* (black belt) grade student. The student is not only expected to continue his growth in the art beyond this level, but also to offer his knowledge to others.

The basic purpose of the test for shodan is to evalauate the candidate in three areas: knowledge of techniques, character, ability, and potential as an instructor. Your knowledge of techniques is the only area of the examination that can be measured objectively based upon the technical skills learned in this book. Your character and ability and your potential as an instructor, can only be measured subjectively based upon an instructor's lengthy observation of you.

If you look at the specific areas of measurement on the Promotion Evaluation Form, you will find that the technical knowledge is only one of the seven specific areas of measurement for the yudansha grades, even though it is weighed twice as heavily as any one of the other six areas.

All of the non-technical areas are measured for a philosophical reason. The examiner assumes you possess technical skill, as that was the emphasis at the brown belt level exam. By the time the student reaches ikkyu he should be technically proficient at all of the techniques presented in this and the first book, as well as somewhat skilled in modifying and varying techniques. At the yudansha level the growth in technical knowledge and skills are still measured (there's still *much* more to learn) but there are now other areas that also must be considered.

The mudansha has reached the stage where he is being examined as a whole person, not just on technical proficiency. Promotions at the yudansha level is based not only on what the candidate knows, but what he is capable of offering and *has* offered to others. The examination approach is different because a shodan is considered *sensei* (an instructor of the art). He is a reflection of his own instructor. A good instructor weighs all of the criteria, general and specific, before promoting an ikkyu to shodan. It's a big step, and one that should be taken with a recognition of all that is involved.

Samples

Promotional examinations for the various kyu and shodan grades in jujitsu appear in the Samples on the following pages. In a normal dojo situation the students are given a copy of the examination as they begin to work for the belt they are striving for. For example, a new student, just starting in the art, would get a copy of the green belt (*rokkyu*) exam at his first class. Once he earned the ranks of rokkyu he would then be given the purple belt (*yonkyu*) exam. This process repeats itself all the way through shodan.

The performance exams are divided into two areas: kata and waza. In the kata portion the student is expected to show specific forms. Increased proficiency is expected at each belt level. To earn rokkyu the student must demonstrate that he can correctly demonstrate most of the basic movements of the required kata. Some of the same kata are tested at each belt level and increased proficiency is required at each level. In the waza portion the student is examined on his ability to react to a variety of attacks. For examination purposes, speed is not essential. The examiner looks to see that the technique is appropriate for the attack. In this section the student is also given freedom to use whatever techniques he knows, whether or not they appear on the kata portion. He may also use some techniques more than once, although excessive repetition (more than two times) of techniques is discouraged.

All of the examinations are used as guides. In a dojo situation it is ultimately up to the instructor as to whether or not the student receives the promotion, even if he passes the technical aspect of the examination. It is the responsibility of the instructor to promote only those students who will serve as good examples in the dojo. In most dojo the sensei informs the student that he would like the student to take a particular belt exam. The student should realize that any promotion in rank is a formal step in his growth in the art. To disregard this aspect of examinations and promotions is to lose an important aspect of the art.

SAMPLE I

SCORING CRITERIA FOR RANK (BELT) EXAMINATIONS

Listed below are the standards used by the AJA for scoring the various belt examinations. Keep in mind this is a guide. The person who is testing you may score in between any of the scores below.

A person taking the green belt examination must average 4.3 on the performance part, assuming they earn a full 28 points on their attitude (ki). A score of five or higher is extremely rare on the green belt examination.

A person taking the purple belt examination must average 4.63 on the performance part, assuming they earn a full 28 points on their attitude. A score higher than five is still rare although there might be a few exceptions.

A person taking any of the brown belt examinations must average 5.25 on the performance part of the test. Your attitude is a major factor in deciding whether you are worthy of the rank you are being considered for.

Score	Criteria
(0)	Unable to execute a technique or wrong technique executed.
(1) Poor	Must be told or shown how technique is done. Barely able to execute technique. Severe loss of balance.
(2) Very Awkward	Very awkward execution of technique. Poor balance. Verbal assistance required. Technique or moves must be repeated at least once.
(3) Barely Effective, Awkward	Somewhat awkward. Poor balance. Some verbal assistance required. Probably repeats or has to repeat moves or technique.
(4) Effective	Technique done fairly smoothly. Little hesitancy in movements. Good balance. No verbal assistance required. No repetition of moves or technique.
(5) Good	Technique done very smoothly. Well balanced. No hesitancy displayed at any time. Return to *tachi waza*. Kiai and/or appropriate submission.
(6) Very Good	Exceptionally good form. Very fluid movement. Execution appears effortless. Kiai and return to *tachi waza*. Submission suitable to technique.
(7) Excellent	Excellent form and execution. Jujitsu as an art.

SAMPLE II

PROMOTION REQUIREMENTS

Progressing in rank is a measurement of growth in jujitsu. In order to earn a promotion in rank you must first demonstrate growth in three areas: physical performance, general knowledge of the art, and your attitude. The chart below outlines the requirements for kyu grade (below black belt) promotions.

RANK	COLORED BELT	PHYSICAL REQUIREMENTS	GENERAL KNOWLEDGE	ATTITUDE
—	White	New student	New student	Desire to learn
Shichikyu (7th kyu)	Yellow belt	80 points (60%) on green belt exam	Green belt requirements	Desire to learn Cooperative
Rokkyu (6th kyu)	Green belt	93 points (70%) on green belt exam	1) Tie obi correctly 2) Show proper method of rolling up gi and tying it formally 3) Know the ten basic situations in which a student is to bow 4) Briefly define jujitsu 5) Count from 1-10 in Japanese	Desire to learn Cooperative
Gokyu (5th kyu)	Green belt with yellow stripe	Exceptional performance on green belt test— approximately 105 points (80%) — or — 74 points on first half of purple belt exam	Green belt requirements Purple belt requirements	Above average attitude Confidence
Shikyu (4th kyu)	Purple belt	191 points (70%) on purple belt exam	1) All green belt requirements 2) Be able to explain proper etiquette in dealing with higher ranks and black belts 3) Explain the differences between judo, karate, aikido and jujitsu	Positive attitude Desire to learn Helpful to lower ranking students
Senior Purple	Purple belt with white stripe	Holding rank between 4th and 3rd kyu. Sometimes issued for various reasons, (e.g., age, maturity, encouragement) until sensei feels criteria for sankyu can be met.		
Sankyu (3rd kyu)	Brown belt with green stripe	131 points (75%) on brown belt exam	1) All green and purple belt requirements 2) Show sensitive points and nerve centers on human body. 3) Explain the philosophy of jujitsu 4) Explain the relative advantages and disadvantages of judo, karate, aikido and jujitsu.	Sets positive example for lower ranks Assists in instructional program
Nikyu (2nd kyu)	Brown belt with black stripe	Above plus evidence of development of an effective and personalized system of self-defense		
Ikkyu (1st kyu)	Brown belt with blue stripe	See above	1) All above requirements 2) Certification as mat referee	Potential as an instructor

SAMPLE III

Student's Name _____ Number_____ Date_____

BROWN BELT PROMOTIONAL EXAMINATION

A student may be able to pass the examination after a minimum of 50-100 hours (6-12 months) active participation in the program as a purple belt.

You must demonstrate ten forms and 15 defenses from the list below, selected at the time of the test. Your reaction to the attacks must be IMMEDIATE. You will be expected to know the names of the forms in Japanese and execute them without delay.

Scoring is as follows: (7) excellent; (6) very good; (5) good; (4) effective; (3) barely effective; (2) very awkward; (1) poor; (0) unable to execute. You must score 131 points (75%) in order to pass this portion of the examination.

KATA (FORMS) (10 selected)

Koshi Nage .... _____
Tai Otoshi .... _____
Ura Nage .... _____
Ouchi Gari .... _____
Shioku Waza .... _____
Te Nage .... _____
Te Tatake .... _____
Ippon Seoi Nage .... _____
Harai Goshi .... _____
Hane Goshi .... _____
Tomoe Nage .... _____
Uki Otoshi .... _____
Yubi Nage .... _____
Makikomi .... _____
Ude Guruma .... _____
Ude Guruma Makikomi .... _____
Ude Guruma Ushiro .... _____
Osoto Gari .... _____
Kubi Nage .... _____
Te Waza .... _____
Ashi Waza .... _____
Hiji Waza .... _____
Shimi Waza .... _____
Hiki Waza .... _____
Tekubi Shimi Waza .... _____

TOTAL KATA .... _____
TOTAL WAZA .... _____

TOTAL SCORE .... _____

WAZA (TECHNIQUES) (15 selected)

Single Hit (left or right, high or low) .... _____
Mugging Attack .... _____
Club Attack (various) .... _____
Kicks .... _____
Handholds (single, double, front and rear) .... _____
Headlock .... _____
Armlock .... _____
Reversing a Throw .... _____
Being Pulled (forward, backward, sideways) .... _____
Football Tackle .... _____
Double Hits .... _____
Hair Grabs (various) .... _____
Knife Attacks (various) .... _____
Lapel Grabs (single or double) .... _____
Combination holds and attacks .... _____
Cross Choke .... _____
Multiple Attackers (usually two) .... _____
Bearhugs and Waistgrabs (arm free or pinned, high or low) .... _____
Nelsons (front and rear) .... _____
Knife Threat .... _____
Chokes (various) .... _____
Handshakes .... _____
Baton Attacks .... _____
Reversing Opponent on Mat .... _____
Shoulder Grabs (front and rear) .... _____
Misc. Clothing Grabs .... _____
Ground Defenses .... _____

COMMENTS: _____
_____
_____

In addition to securing a passing score you must also have demonstrated a positive attitude toward the art and the class. If you are being examined for Ikkyu your examiner will also consider your potential as an instructor. Your examiner will be looking to see if you are developing a coherent style, suited to your physical stature, condition and agility.

If you pass the brown belt exam and the instructor feels that you are qualified to receive a brown belt, a Certificate of Promotion will be issued.

SAMPLE IV

REQUEST FOR CONSIDERATION FOR PROMOTION (YUDANSHA)
BUDOSHIN JUJITSU

Your Name _____ Address _____
Date of exam for_____ Dan _____ City _____ State _____ Zip_____
Instructor _____ Dojo _____
Age_____ Education level _____ Occupation _____
Current rank_____ Date promoted to current rank_____
How long teaching? (shodan & up) _____ In your dojo? Yes_____No_____
If instructing in another dojo please name instructor & dojo: _____

Provide the following information to the best of your ability. Answers should be handwritten or typed. Please make sure that your answers are complete.

I. Candidates for *shodan* should answer questions 1-9 below:

1. What is the philosophy of jujitsu? Explain yourself fully.
2. What responsibilities should a person of the rank you are applying for have toward (a) your instructor, (b) your dojo, (c) the AJA, and (d) the art of jujitsu?
3. What will you offer your dojo as a _____dan?
4. Do you want to be an instructor? What makes you think you'd be a good instructor? Give some reasons for your answer. (If you do not wish to instruct please explain.)
5. Have you assumed any responsibilities in your dojo? Please list and describe them.
6. Do you feel that you can assume responsibility without constant supervision? Please give some examples in which you demonstrated independent judgment or the ability to rely solely on yourself.
7. What is your definition of the word "disipline?" What would you do if someone disobeyed you?
8. Do you feel comfortable working in a tightly disciplined organization in which you also give directions and expect them to be carried out? Please explain your answer fully.
9. Is there anything you would like to add that would help in your evaluation? Is there anything that has prevented you from meeting any of the requirements of the rank you are applying for?

II. Candidates for nidan & higher grades should answer #1, 2 & 9 above as well as comment on your experience(s) in the three areas below, detailed in Section IV of the National Black Belt Board Criteria for Promotion:

(A) Personal growth in the martial arts
(B) Potential for future growth
(C) Contributions to the dojo, AJA, and the art

Your responses on these three areas should be as complete as possible and in essay or outline format.

The candidate named above has my permission to be considered for promotion to the rank of _____. This application is complete and correct.

_____
Instructor's signature

SAMPLE V

PROMOTION EVALUATION FORM — YUDANSHA

Candidate's name _____
Date _____ Current rank _____
Examiner's name _____

To the Candidate: You will be graded in each of the areas listed below. All questions will be asked of you and answered by you while you are on the mat. Please be aware that the examination is a very formal event.

AREA OF EVALUATION:	SCORE:	EXAMINER'S COMMENTS:
I. Theory, history and philosophy (based upon recommended reading and instruction) Score range: 1-5 (1 = poor, 5 = excellent)	_____	
II Application of theory (e.g. explanation and use of ki, circle theory, etc., from reading and instruction) Score range: 1-5	_____	
III. Measurement of continuing growth (involvement in workshops, continued instruction and/or technical growth) Score range: 1-5	_____	
IV. Contributions to art and the organization (responsibilities assumed, refer to Request for Consideration Form attached) Score range: 1-5	_____	
V. Teaching record (refer to formal evaluations attached) Score range: 1-5	_____	
VI. Participation in a support of organization activities (attitude as reflected by own and students' involvement) Score range: 1-5	_____	
VII. Technical knowledge (mat examination score will be converted to the nearest whole number on a scale of 1-10) Score range: 1-10	_____	

(Continue on back if more space is needed)

Total Score: _____ 31 + required

SHODAN TECHNICAL KNOWLEDGE/MAT EXAMINATION

The purpose of a mat examination is to determine your proficiency in the physical aspects of the art. The requirements below are general guidelines that will be followed for the shodan examination. The mat examination will determine about 25 percent of your total evaluation score. It is very important that you do well in this area.

The mat examination for all yudansha grades below godan is based upon the brown belt examination. You will be expected to demonstrate at least two variations of each kata. The variation must be in the actual execution of the requested kata. You must also be able to show a loosening up maneuver and submission (hold, pin, strike, come-along, etc.) whenever possible. Jujitsu techniques should be *complete.* On the waza portion you should be able to demonstrate two to three defenses for each type of attack. You performance should average 5.4 or higher based upon the seven-point scale on all kyu-grade examinations. On the average you can expect about five kata and five waza, not including variations.

You should be aware that many of the techniques requested on the kata portion of the test are generic terms. There might be several types of koshi nage, shimi waza, te nage, uki otoshi, etc., that you could do. You would be able to select the specific technique in such cases unless the examiner specifies a specific kata.

GLOSSARY

Index of Techniques

Generic Terminology

You will notice that some terms have several different techniques after them. They may or may not be called the same in English. For example, there are six *ude guruma* listed, each of which are different (sometimes just slightly), yet they all go by the same name. There are also eight *shimi waza* listed that are different techniques.

Also, there are some techniques that have the phrase shimi waza in them; e.g. *tekubi* shimi waza, *ube* shimi waza, *eri* shimi waza. Any of these strangling or pain techniques could be demonstrated on the brown or black belt examinations if shimi waza was requested by the examiner. The same idea would apply if the examiner asked for a *koshi nage* (hip throw). Any type of hip throw would be allowed as there are many variations of the basic technique. Page locations are listed after translations.

* Actual definition of Japanese term but no techniques specifically listed here under the definitive term.
† Page to be found in **Jujitsu: Basic Techniques of the Gentle Art** *(Ohara Publications).*